Advance Praise for
Divided We Stand: The Search for America's Soul

"No matter the political party, there is always that person who knows the lay of the land and has the ear of key influencers and the policy makers. One of those persons is Dr. Chris Metzler. His understanding of what is happening, and what happened, and what will happen is far and above the rest."

—APRIL D. RYAN, CNN Political Analyst

"*Divided We Stand* is a perspective from a Caribbean-born American who recognizes the transformation from 'America,' the land of the free, to 'Merica,' the land where some are restricted to be free. Dr. Metzler is one of those who refuses to stay on the sidelines to see Americans and America become more polarized and spiral into a country that may become unrecognizable from that which our Forefathers created. It's now wake-up time and Dr. Metzler's insights will light the fire."

—JENNIFER SANDRA CARROLL, Retired Naval Office
and former Lieutenant Governor of Florida

"*Divided We Stand* is an exploration of the issues that polarize America. Dr. Metzler throws political correctness out the window in his conservative critique punching to the left and the right of American politics. No matter where you stand to the left or to the right of center, Dr. Metzler's book will be an electrifying read."

—DEBORAH P. ASHTON, Ph.D., CDM (aka Dr. Deb)

DIVIDED WE STAND:
THE SEARCH
FOR AMERICA'S SOUL

DIVIDED WE STAND:
THE SEARCH
FOR AMERICA'S SOUL

DR. CHRISTOPHER J. METZLER

A POST HILL PRESS BOOK

Divided We Stand:
The Search for America's Soul
© 2019 by Dr. Christopher J. Metzler
All Rights Reserved

ISBN: 978-1-68261-821-9
ISBN (eBook): 978-1-68261-822-6

Cover Art by Cody Corcoran

Post Hill Press
New York • Nashville
posthillpress.com

Published in the United States of America

DEDICATION

I learned to read at the age of two because of my maternal grandmother, Monica Charles. A broadcaster and government official, she knew what the future would be. It started off with her giving me several names—among them, Fitzgerald (of Kennedy fame). Although cancer claimed her life at a relatively young age, she inspired me greatly and continues to look down on me from Heaven daily.

My parents, Kenneth and Ingrid Metzler, are my solid and unwavering rocks. From them, I learned the power of reasoning, how to make informed choices, and that I am owed nothing. I eat what I kill. Their endless and selfless dedication to self-sufficiency is nourishment to my soul.

CONTENTS

CHAPTER 1

The Panic Button:
Facing America's Biggest Fears

As an emigrant from the tiny nation of Grenada, I arrived in St. Thomas, U.S. Virgin Islands, at seven years old and in Florida at ten years old. Upon becoming an American citizen, I found America to be a happy country. In my Florida community, the police talked often with parents and children to ensure that children followed the law, respected the police, and learned from their mistakes. In those days (the 1970s), the police protected and served. They were part of the community. Crime was minimal and happened largely in communities that lacked law and order, or where there was a high degree of absent parents. Issues of race discrimination, brutal confrontations, and isolated neighbors were rare. This is not to suggest that these problems did not exist; however, in my experience, people were *American* first. Identifying as American was the thread that kept us together. In my community, we were not a hyphenated people—for example, African-American, Asian-American, and so forth. This does not mean that we did not celebrate our heritage; it just meant that we were happy Americans.

Today, in contrast, America is an angry place. Many American communities are no longer intact. People are sharply divided by race, class, education, gender, and political affiliation. People no longer speak respectfully to one another; instead, they name-call, shout one another down, bully one another, and revel in the politics of personal destruction.

To be sure, America's decline into the dark and ugly abyss whose pungent, repugnant odor continues to eat away at the base of the republic did not happen only recently; it started with societal changes that sought to recognize the racial and ethnic diversity that was becoming a reality in America. This chapter will explore some of the issues facing a sharply divided America. America is a country like no other. People want to come here because of how free we are and the greatness of the republic. Yet this country is deeply divided. The division is based on the reality that the left has hijacked the national discourse with help from the media, the courts, and elites whose version of the soul of the republic is simply out of touch with reality. The result is strife and discord within the republic. We cannot allow this to continue. Taking back our country is not a slogan; it is a matter of national security.

Anger Over Equal Rights, Affirmative Action, and Welfare Benefits

The Civil Rights Act of 1964 angered many whites who thought that since slavery as a practice had been dissolved, there was no need to make what they thought of as special laws to protect blacks. And many white men who traditionally worked in factories and police departments and who belonged to unions started to believe that they and generations to come would lose all of what they and generations to come were entitled to. They were angry.

In addition to signing the Civil Rights Act of 1964, President Lyndon B. Johnson signed Executive Order 11246, which called for affirmative action in government contracting. Under this executive order, any business that wanted to do business with the federal government had to take action to remedy past discrimination, correct present discrimination, and prevent future discrimination. Of course, a business could simply opt out of affirmative action by not bidding on federal government contracts. However, given the behemoth size, scope, and monetary value that federal government contracting provides, very few businesses opted out. Yet they still complained about affirmative action.

For many whites, the issue was employment. In their view, affirmative action required that "unqualified" blacks be hired to displace them in staggering numbers. Many employers were complicit in keeping this myth alive by hiring blacks who were unqualified to do the jobs they were hired to do. Employers choosing this path also stoked the flames of racism by stating that affirmative action required quotas and that they had to hire blacks regardless of their qualifications. In fact, the law explicitly prohibited hiring people just because they were black.

Black activists such as the Reverend Al Sharpton and the Reverend Jesse Jackson also bear responsibility for fanning the racial flames while enriching their own pockets. Both Jackson and Sharpton formed organizations designed to advance the "black agenda." The problem here is that they both used these organizations to "shake down" corporations by threatening boycotts and pickets if they were not paid for their services in getting communities to keep quiet. They both became poverty pimps, which further exacerbated racial tensions.

In addition to the Civil Rights Act and employment changes, many whites became increasingly angry about welfare, which in their minds was designed to use their tax dollars to bolster "lazy blacks," who would live off the government dole and raise generations on welfare. Of course, they failed to admit that there were many whites on welfare as well. Confronted with this reality, many argued—and still do argue—that, as a percentage of the population, there are more blacks on welfare. This is true.

In my view, however, the issue is not welfare as a concept. It is, instead, how the system was designed and implemented. There is nothing wrong with helping people who need help to get on their feet. This help, however, should be limited in time and scope, and its end game should be helping people to help themselves. The current system is designed and implemented to keep recipients trapped in poverty, because there is no end game; generations remain on welfare for the foreseeable future, and many will never become fully productive members of American society.

Divisiveness Over Gun Laws and the Right to Bear Arms

The anger is not limited to race, either. It includes the Second Amendment to the Constitution and gun laws. I simply cannot understand why Democrats, progressives, and others cannot concede, once and for all, that the right to bear arms is protected by the Constitution. Period. Instead, they go on and on about the definition of "militia," the influence of the National Rifle Association, and the gun lobby. To be clear, every interest group has a lobbying organization, so that is not the issue. They ought to realize that Congress can impose reasonable regulations regarding the Second Amendment, as it has done. When so many people hear the endless jockeying about guns and gun rights, the anger becomes even more pronounced.

Anger at the Government

For many people, Washington itself is also a source of deep-seated anger. Many believe that the government in Washington is not working on behalf of the people who have sent the politicians there to work for them.

Yet while Washington is such a cesspool, the people directing anger toward it have done very little to change the players. There was a brief rebellion with the tea party, but that ended in disaster because many of those elected were part of the problem. In many cases, angry Americans are themselves to blame, because they elect people to office and simply do not hold them accountable. They have allowed political parties to control the sum and substance of policy-making, and they rarely throw them out of office. Anger without action means nothing. In fact, it is an emotional response that is not new to D.C. at all. Politicians simply ignore the anger because they know that the electorate will soon move onto something else and or they "feel your pain" as former President Clinton said.

It is the hypnosis of the angry that keeps Washington the way it is. The angry can continue to be angry at Washington as much as they want to, but Washington will exhaust them before elected officials change their behavior.

The Media Divide: News Is No Longer Neutral

The American media has become a deeply partisan source of news. Stations seek out conservative, liberal, and/or progressive views when covering news. The proliferation of contributors has become nauseating. When booking talking heads, the bookers, producers, and hosts often seek to create good television by placing liberals against conservatives, in the hope that they will clash and the result will be reality TV and not education. Many of the talking heads are shock jocks who use catchy phrases to increase ratings. There is no more debate and disagreement with the goal of education. Instead, the media is a train wreck.

I know from personal experience that bringing a principled, informed viewpoint as a pundit is not valued. I was once contacted about potentially being a guest on an MSNBC show. I spoke at length with the booker about my views on the policies of the Trump administration. Since those views did not fit the MSNBC narrative, I was not booked. As I am a black conservative, many of the networks will not book me unless I stand clearly with their views of what a conservative should look like and how a conservative should act and behave. Why? Because they want to create a minstrel show in which I appear unreasonable and the white liberals can attack me with wanton abandon.

Many people who are angry with the media feel that the media is responsible for creating racial division, for silencing conservative voices, for being anti-white, for being anti-Christian, and for decrying the liberals' takeover of America. The media, in their view, has normalized homosexuality, glorified single motherhood, emasculated men, and disrespected traditional American values. They are seething at the so-called mainstream media. Thus, they have turned to the musings of so-called conservative media. Talk radio, for many of them, has become a welcome respite. They also have followed ultraconservative pundits such as Rush Limbaugh (himself a drug addict), the bombastic Sean Hannity, and the hard-questioning and highly opinionated Bill O'Reilly. For Dick and Debbie Salt of the Earth, these outlets provide facts.

I must point out here, though, that these outlets provide *opinion* with a sprinkling of facts, much like the mainstream media does. But, just like liberals and so-called progressives, these outlets simply think like the audience they attract and are careless about reporting facts.

Supreme Court Cases and Decisions that Have Widened the Divide

During Earl Warren's third term as governor of California, President Dwight D. Eisenhower, a moderate conservative, nominated Warren in 1953 to be chief justice of the U.S. Supreme Court, stating, "He represents the kind of political, economic, and social thinking that I believe we need on the Supreme Court." Warren quickly won legislative approval and became the court's leading judge, succeeding the late Fred Vinson.

In the next few years, Warren led the court in a series of liberal decisions that transformed the role of the U.S. Supreme Court. Warren was considered a judicial activist, in that he believed the Constitution should be interpreted based on the times. Eisenhower later remarked that his appointment was "the biggest damned-fool mistake I ever made." As chief justice, Warren spearheaded radical changes in areas of equal protection, law enforcement, and representative apportionment.

Warren helped end school segregation with the court's decision in *Brown v. Board of Education* (1954). The Fourteenth Amendment didn't clearly disallow segregation, and the doctrine of "separate but equal" was deemed constitutional in the 1896 case of *Plessy v. Ferguson*. However, the Plessy decision pertained to transportation, not education. In his written opinion, Warren stated that "in the field of public education, the doctrine of 'separate but equal' has no place. Separate educational facilities are inherently unequal." The Warren court was largely responsible for eliminating segregation as a matter of law. That is, the court examined ways in which the law encouraged and even rewarded segregation. This was a much-needed start. However, it was not within the purview of the court to implement these policies among the several states. While the court made it clear to the states that segregation was unconstitutional, it was up to the states to ensure that discrimination was not occurring in the states. Thus, states enacted legislation prohibiting discrimination. At the time, race was the issue. More specifically, the issue was about blacks, because blacks made up the largest population enslaved in America. Also, this discrimination resulted in the creation of stereotypes that advantaged whites and disadvantaged blacks.

During its tenure, the Warren court generated a seismic shift in the area of criminal justice procedure. As a result of discrimination, the courts were very tough on blacks. Criminal justice procedure generally begins with a formal criminal charge and results in the conviction or acquittal of the defendant. The Warren court found that the procedure, when applied to blacks, was discriminatory and so needed significant change.

Beginning in 1961, the case of *Mapp v. Ohio* questioned whether credible evidence obtained through an illegal search could be admissible in court. In 1914, the Supreme Court ruled in *Weeks v. United States* that evidence illegally obtained could not be used in federal court. However, that ruling did not extend to the states. In 1961, the Warren court ruled that illegally obtained evidence was not admissible in state courts due to the Fourteenth Amendment's due-process clause. Subsequent court rulings have created some exceptions to this ruling, but its main intent remains in force.

In one of its more personal cases affecting the lives of ordinary people, the Warren court took on state anti-miscegenation laws banning interracial marriage in the case of *Loving v. Virginia* (1967). Mildred and Richard Loving were married in Virginia but soon were convicted of violating the law against interracial marriage. They fled to Washington, D.C., for a few years, but then returned to Virginia. The Lovings were arrested, found guilty, and sentenced to a year in jail. Inspired by the Johnson administration's fight for civil rights, Mildred Loving wrote a letter to then attorney general Robert Kennedy, who advised the couple to contact the American Civil Liberties Union.

Two of its lawyers represented the Lovings at the Supreme Court. In a unanimous decision, the court ruled that anti-miscegenation laws were unconstitutional under the Equal Protection Clause of the Fourteenth Amendment.

In 1966, the Warren court made another controversial ruling on criminal justice procedure in the case of *Miranda v. Arizona*. In a close (five-to-four) decision, the court ruled that a suspect must be informed of his or her rights to remain silent and have counsel at the time of arrest, or the arrest and all the evidence obtained are inadmissible in court. The reality was that blacks were not informed of their rights based on anything other than the color of their skin.

While Earl Warren was chief justice, the court also dealt with state-sponsored discrimination though apportionment of legislative districts. While in theory, voting was the right of any freeman, the states often made it impossible for blacks to elect people who would have their best interests at heart. It was the practice of many states, despite rulings outlawing discrimination by the courts, to make the right to vote almost impossible to enact.

For decades, the state of Alabama had used the 1900 census to apportion representation in state legislative districts. Since then, the population had shifted from rural to urban areas. The greater population in the urban areas (primarily African-Americans and other minorities) was disproportionately represented because the state used the older census. In *Reynolds v. Sims* (1964), the court ruled that Alabama had to reapportion its state legislative districts based on current population figures. Writing for the court, chief justice Earl Warren argued that the right to vote freely and unimpaired preserved all the other basic civil and political rights.

This made Dick and Debbie Salt of the Earth angry with the court. They believed (and rightly so) that the justices made law, which was outside their purview. The court is supposed to interpret, not make, law. For Dick and Debbie, this was not merely an academic question; it affected their lives in profound ways. Other examples were *Roe v. Wade*, the abortion case, and the case that decided marriage between people of the same sex was constitutional and thus legal.

Many conservatives considered the Warren court to be liberal and permissive. That liberal nature led, in many of their minds, to the decision in *Roe v. Wade*.

The Warren court is despised by many conservatives.

"The justices first jettisoned Court precedent that had held reapportionment questions beyond the reach of the federal courts. This was the Baker v. Carr (1962) decision, holding that individual voters could raise a challenge to malapportionment under the Fourteenth Amendment. Two years later, the justices forged a novel legal standard—"one person, one vote"—under which anything short of a near parity of populations between voting districts was deemed to violate the equal protection clause of the Fourteenth Amendment. In astoundingly short order, the Court overturned the voting arrangements of practically every state in the union."[1]

In addition to race, abortion is one of the most divisive issues in America. It is important to set forth the genesis of the disagreement to paint a full picture of the issues that have divided us during the Warren court and subsequent court decisions. It is only then that we can begin to see how we got here.

Roe v. Wade was a landmark 1973 Supreme Court decision that established a woman's legal right to an abortion. The court ruled, in a seven-to-two decision, that a woman's right to choose an abortion was protected by the privacy rights guaranteed by the Fourteenth Amendment to the U.S. Constitution. The legal precedent for the decision was

---

[1] "The Forgotten Backlash Against the Warren Court," Chris Schmidt, Dec 30, 2014, http://www.blogs.kentlaw.iit.edu/iscotus/forgotten-backlash-warren-court/

rooted in the 1965 case of *Griswold v. Connecticut*, which established the right to privacy involving medical procedures.

Despite opponents' characterization of the decision, it was not the first time that abortion had become a legal procedure in the United States. In fact, for most of the country's first hundred years, abortion as we know it today was not only not a criminal offense but also was not considered immoral.

In the 1700s and early 1800s, the word "abortion" referred only to the termination of a pregnancy after "quickening," the time when the fetus first begins to make noticeable movements. The induced ending of a pregnancy before this point did not even have a name—but not because it was uncommon. Women in the 1700s often took drugs to end their unwanted pregnancies.

In 1827, though, Illinois passed a law that made the use of abortion drugs punishable by up to three years' imprisonment. Although other states followed the Illinois example, advertising for "female monthly pills," as they were known, was still common through the middle of the nineteenth century.

Abortion itself only became a serious criminal offense between 1860 and 1880. And the criminalization of abortion was not due to moral outrage. The roots of the new law came from the newly established physicians' trade organization, the American Medical Association. Doctors decided that abortion practitioners were unwanted competition and went about eliminating that competition.

The Catholic Church, which had long accepted terminating pregnancies before quickening, joined the doctors in condemning the practice.

By the turn of the twentieth century, all states had laws against abortion, but for the most part they were rarely enforced, and women with money had no problem terminating pregnancies if they wished. It wasn't until the late 1930s that abortion laws were enforced. Subsequent crackdowns led to a reform movement that succeeded in lifting abortion restrictions in California and New York even before the Supreme Court decision in *Roe v. Wade*.

The fight over whether to criminalize abortion has grown increasingly fierce in recent years, but opinion polls suggest that most Americans prefer that women be able to have abortions in the early stages of pregnancy, free of any government interference.

For many conservatives, *Roe* was devastating. It dealt a serious blow to what in their view is a bedrock principle of conservatism: protection for the sanctity of human life. *Roe* ruled that women could abort unborn babies. Many considered it homicide and erupted in anger against the court. They felt the court was packed with judges who are not elected to any position by the citizens of America. Instead, at the federal level, they have lifetime appointments and are not accountable to anyone. However, as in the case of Roe, they made a decision that affects all of our lives. Understanding this, conservatives turned their attention to the importance of electing a president who accepts conservatism and a Senate who would confirm conservative judges.

Judges were considered elitist academics who looked down their noses at Dick and Debbie and considered them to be uneducated country bumpkins.

Anger About Illegal Immigration

I focused the first part of this chapter on blacks because I was dealing with a historical context. But the issue of Latinos, and particularly illegal immigrants from Mexico, soon became a crucial part of the anger that I have written about. This book is not politically correct, and so I will not use the terms "African-Americans" and "undocumented immigrants." It is simply my prerogative as the author.

America was founded on the principles of diversity and acceptance, including accepting immigrants into the country. While both major political parties agree on continuing to support immigration,[2] they disagree on what to do about those who enter the country by any way but the accepted method. Republican views on illegal immigration are comparably intolerant. Republicans believe that illegal immigrants are taking jobs, seats in schools, and tax dollars from legal citizens who have paid into the system their entire lives.

Many Republicans also believe that illegal immigrants contribute to higher crime rates. This belief stems from the idea that these people have broken the law in coming into the country, and therefore have shown a predisposition toward criminal activity. Republicans are strongly against amnesty for those who have come here illegally, and they also hope to see systems developed that will punish employers who knowingly hire illegal immigrants. They believe that illegal immigrants should be deported when caught, and that border security should be a high priority of the government so as to prevent more illegal immigrants from entering the country.

Democrats believe that illegal immigrants contribute greatly to the American economy. In their view, there are jobs that Americans do not want to do, and illegals can fill those jobs. They also believe that you cannot simply throw out all of the illegals currently in this country without doing great harm to the American way of life. In particular, they believe that children who were brought here by their parents without the proper papers should not be penalized. Some Democrats believe in a blanket amnesty program.

The Republican Party strongly believes that providing amnesty to illegal immigrants only further encourages illegal immigration. They also seek stricter penalties for new illegal aliens than for those already

---

[2] "Republicans and Democrats may actually agree about immigration. Why that's not enough." Sean Sullivan, June 20, 2013, https://www.washingtonpost.com/news/the-fix/wp/2013/06/20/republicans-and-democrats-may-actually-agree-about-immigration-why-thats-not-enough/?utm_term=.80d0c52f7092

in place, and would like stricter laws against those who help smuggle illegal aliens into the country, those who create fraudulent documents to prolong the ability of illegal aliens to stay in the country, and employers who knowingly hire illegal aliens. They also support the right of border patrol agents to deport illegal immigrants without giving them a hearing before a judge. They argue that illegal immigrants' disregard for American laws negates their right to a trial, which should be reserved for citizens who pay tax dollars into the legal system.

The party has stuck to these beliefs even when it has meant opposing other members of their party. In the book *2004 Republican Party Platform*, the party spoke out against President George W. Bush's plan to implement a new temporary worker program that would allow those working as illegal aliens to apply for citizenship the same way as those applying from outside the country. The party platform argued that Bush's proposal would only deter those applying from outside the country from going through the proper channels. Republicans stated that this measure would provide unfair advantages to those who had broken our laws and would put them on a par with those who were working hard to obey the law.

Democrats view immigration policy as an opportunity to renew the "American community." What this means is unclear. Understanding the political implications, the modern-day Democratic platform on immigration mentions the importance of border security's using several means, including physical and technological. They do not wish to appear soft on security. They also discuss the need to enforce existing laws. The platform mentions "comprehensive immigration reform," which seems to suggest that this can all be fixed, despite its nuances and complexities, in one bill. Noticeably absent from the party's platform is any reference to the controversial border fence. Rather, "comprehensive" immigration reform remains a top priority for Democrats.

Specifically, the Democrats' plan calls for increasing family-based and employment-based immigrant visas, improving the naturalization process, and addressing the dysfunctional immigration bureaucracy. Moreover, the Democratic platform supports a path for undocumented immigrants to become legal permanent residents, or in their words, to "get right with the law." Indeed, Democrats "support a system that requires undocumented immigrants who are in good standing to pay a fine, pay taxes, learn English, and go to the back of the line for the opportunity to become citizens."

Anger at Obamacare

Perhaps nothing has angered conservatives more than the enactment of Obamacare (the official name is the Patient Protection and Affordable Care Act, or ACA). The anger is in part based on the fact that this was the second attempt to have government take control of a massive, expensive, and forced approach to healthcare. When Hillary Clinton was the first lady, she made a disastrous attempt to "reform" healthcare. Conservatives correctly rejoiced at its demise. The Heritage Foundation said:

> *"In 1993, after heading up a 500-member task force on health-care that worked behind closed doors for months, Hillary Clinton produced a 1,342-page monster. This mammoth prescription for health reform collapsed of its own weight and helped to bring down a Democratic Congress one year later. In a sharp reversal of historical trends, the Clinton Administration and congressional Democrats had lost public trust on the healthcare issue."*[3]

Many simply did not like the idea that government would be in control of our healthcare system. Americans have long memories, and

---

[3] "HillaryCare II: A Big Leap in Federal Control," Robert E. Moffit, Ph.D., Sept. 25, 2007, https://www.heritage.org/health-care-reform/commentary/hillarycare-ii-big-leap-federal-control

so when the president proposed "reforming healthcare," many balked. That balking turned to anger.

According to the Department of Health and Human Services (HHS):

> *"The Affordable Care Act (ACA) is the name for the comprehensive healthcare reform law and its amendments. The law addresses health insurance coverage, healthcare costs, and preventive care. The law was enacted in two parts: The Patient Protection and Affordable Care Act was signed into law on March 23, 2010 and was amended by the Health Care and Education Reconciliation Act on March 30, 2010."[4]*

Sounds innocent enough. But wait, the anger is about what this definition does not tell us. First, the act included a penalty (since repealed) for people who did not have health insurance. Second, it was written in large part by lobbyists and health insurance companies who had an interest in its outcome. Third, it did not cover everyone. Fourth, it drove the costs of premiums higher, and President Barack Obama misled the public into thinking that the bill was not a tax bill; he later admitted in court filings that it was in fact a tax-raising bill.

While pitching Obamacare in 2009, President Obama said that "we will keep this promise to the American people: if you like your doctor, you will be able to keep your doctor, period. If you like your healthcare plan, you'll be able to keep your healthcare plan, period."[5]

Four years later, this frequently repeated claim was rated the "Lie of the Year" and was characterized as an "unfulfillable blanket promise" that was "impossible to keep."[6]

---

[4] "Affordable Care Act (ACA)," https://www.healthcare.gov/glossary/affordable-care-act/

[5] "Obama's pledge that 'no one will take away' your health plan," https://www.washington post.com/news/fact-checker/wp/2013/10/30/obamas-pledge-that-no-one-will-take-away-your-health-plan/?utm_term=.458f39dc731a

[6] "The Lie Used To Sell Obamacare To America #TBT," https://gop.com/the-lie-used-to-sell-obamacare-to-america-tbt/

Millions of Americans lost their individual plans, and hundreds of employers had to drop their healthcare options for employees when Obamacare provisions kicked in in 2014.

Many people were even forced to change doctors, as insurers and hospitals struggled to determine who would bear the burden of increasing Obamacare costs.

Obamacare problems continue as premiums continue to rise and fewer insurers are able to participate on the healthcare exchanges.[7]

Having already been betrayed by the failed Clinton healthcare bill and then once again getting hit with a less-than-honest representation by the Obama administration, many Americans in all parties became even angrier. A big part of the reason for anger in a divided America is a dishonest government. And Obamacare fit that mold. Healthcare, choice, and taxes are not simply about policy positions for Americans. They affect us and our families in a very personal way. We send elected officials to Washington to represent us, not to mislead us. We are also angry about the influence that lobbyists and big business have on us. So learning how intimately involved they were in helping to craft the healthcare bill angered us even more.

I offer the following quote to help explain the fact that Democratic lawmakers know the power and influence of the insurance lobby over healthcare yet they chose to make the deal with the devil anyway. For them it is more about political survival and less about the health of Americans. Tom Daschle has proven this point in the following statement:

> "In the words of former Senate majority leader Tom Daschle, insurance companies are "not necessarily unbiased. They have a lot of skin in the game." Indeed, one of the more peculiar aspects of the Obamacare debate has been the mainstream media's apparent

---

[7] Ibid.

bemusement at the insurance industry's support for a law that not only forces people to buy its products (which are necessarily more expensive under the law) but also offers direct taxpayer subsidies to help cover the cost, to the tune of nearly $500 billion over the next ten years.

It was hardly a shock when, in 2011, the industry's largest lobbying group, America's Health Insurance Plans, argued in an amicus brief to the Supreme Court that, in the event that the individual mandate to purchase insurance was struck down, Obamacare should be scrapped entirely."[8]

But this anger is not just about healthcare. It is also about corruption, self-dealing, and the increasing role that government is playing in our lives. The federal government already has encroached on traditionally state-based jurisdictions, such as public education, with catastrophic results, and so many correctly believed that Obamacare would be no different. The idea of government control of healthcare is not a new one, nor is the disaster that occurs when we cede absolute control of our healthcare to the government. One simply needs to look at the United Kingdom and Canada, where one will find rationing, healthcare cuts, and other woes. The anger was based on the fact that many thought Obama wanted to create a legacy of healthcare reform based on a house of cards.

I work in the field of healthcare and politics every day. On the healthcare side, I own and operate several medical businesses in the state of Florida which saw a loss of revenue because many people simply could not afford their share of health care costs.

It is important to educate consumers about the rise of PBMs, because a PBM impacts the cost of your insurance greatly. A PBM is a pharmacy benefit company which is unregulated. As the owner of

---

[8] "Obamacare and Its Cronies," Andrew Stiles, *National Review Online*, Dec 3, 2013, https://www.nationalreview.com/2013/12/obamacare-and-its-cronies-andrew-stiles/

a pharmacy, I have to purchase drugs for my patients in advance. For example, I purchase Medicine X for twelve hundred dollars per dose. I then bill the insurance company of the patient. Because PBMs are unregulated, they can pay me whatever they want to for that drug thus causing an increase in the cost of healthcare. It may mean, for example, that I may have to decide not to fill that prescription or find a way to recoup the cost in another way.

Here are, in my experience, some of their deceptive tactics:

- Classifying certain generic drugs as brand drugs and charging brand prices.
- Promoting drugs by telling consumers that if they choose certain drugs, they will get a rebate. This is an attractive selling point. However, what they don't disclose is that PBM obtains those rebates based on the amount of money it gets from the drug company which is not necessarily in the consumer's best interest. PBMs have a love affair with brands from which they get the highest rebate, even if there is an equally-well or better-suited drug that is cheaper for the consumer. Sometimes PBMs will even switch patients' prescriptions without the knowledge of the patient, just so that the PBM can receive the rebate.
- Utilizing spread pricing by charging health plans more than they reimburse pharmacies, and pocketing the difference.
- Using abusive audit practices and penalizing pharmacies for minor, typographical errors on claims, forcing them to forego reimbursement due to small errors that posed no consequence to the claim. This practice targets small independent, community pharmacies which some Americans use to get their medicines. The result is that many of these pharmacies will have to choose to go out of business or serve the consumer.

In the political arena, I spend time conducting focus groups about the cost of healthcare. What Americans hated the most about Obamacare was the fact that the President was less than honest in selling it to the American people, that the President failed to disclose that Obamacare was a tax and that the costs of healthcare went up not down. Finally, they did not like the fact that Obamacare was just another form of big government. Government can't even run the post office effectively yet Obama wanted us to trust them with running healthcare?

The following quote explains why so many Americans were angry about Obamacare. To many of them it was not only about promises made, it was also about lying to the American people:

> *"In 2013, millions discovered that the "keep your plan" promise was a lie—PolitiFact gave it the "Lie of the Year" award—when they started getting cancellation notices from their insurers. The Obama administration scrambled to minimize the political fallout by letting some keep those plans.*
>
> *While Obama repeatedly promised a premium cut thanks to improved efficiency in the healthcare system, the opposite occurred. Workplace premiums for family plans jumped 9.4% the year after ObamaCare became law, and rose $4,767 from 2009 to 2006. ObamaCare premiums are going up at double-digit rates."*[9]

Conclusion

Yes, America is an angry place and it is a divided place. It is a place that is still searching for its soul. The anger is easily understood given the issues I have raised. Americans have a streak of independence that

---

[9] "Unlike ObamaCare, The GOP Health Bill Wasn't Built On Lies And False Promises," May 5, 2017, https://www.investors.com/politics/editorials/unlike-obamacare-the-gop-health-bill-wasnt -built-on-lies-and-false-promises/

we hold on to for dear life. It is this streak that drives our political and cultural discussions. In the past few decades, activist courts, political correctness, corrupt politicians, and a government that isn't working have driven us into tribes rather than made us united Americans. In those tribes, we feel best expressing our anger with like-minded people. The tribes provide us with a sense of safety and security that an increasingly detached and disinterested government cannot.

Many commentators have blamed an angry America for the election of Donald Trump. Many party activists have painted him as being racist, sexist, and a homophobe. Rather than the commentators realizing the reason for an angry America, they shifted their own anger to Trump as the cause of such anger. In modern times and within the Republican Party, The Tea Party wielded tremendous power and disrupted much of traditional Washington and the Republican and Democratic parties. The Tea Party is based on anger about government overreaching, excessive taxation and permissive immigration policies. They expressed their anger by taking to the streets and through a grassroots strategy involving ordinary Americans worked to defeat any elected official who did not support their agenda and replace them with ones who did.

American anger is nothing new, and the proverbial chatter about Trump's being an angry white man is simply just rubbish. I suggest that we try to understand the reasons for the anger and how this anger has led to a "house divided against itself." Unless we make sustained and disruptive change, anger will not end with Donald Trump. It may, however, be the emotion that leads us further and further toward the point of no return.

Donald Trump did not create an angry America; he simply harnessed that anger to get elected. He realized that angry voters had anger that was both identity- and value-based. So many of the people who elected him had a vision of the American dream that they thought would never be realized, and so they turned to Trump to help that dream become a reality.

In this book, I will explore the reasons America is such an angry place by focusing on some of the most divisive issues in America, along with how the anger affects the nation as a whole. My goal is simple: to present the issues and my analysis to help you decide for yourself the impact of those issues. Yes, this book is written from my experience with the issues and from a conservative point of view, because I am a conservative. People will take away different things from my writing, and I am fine with that. This book presents an opportunity for all Americans to reflect on their place in a divided America. It is by no means the definitive book on the issues. It is instead a contribution to the analyses of the size and scope of the issues in a divided America.

CHAPTER 2

Political Correctness:
A Stain on America's Soul

After emigrating from Grenada and living in St. Thomas in the U.S. Virgin Islands, I grew up in Fort Lauderdale, Florida. South Florida is a great place weather-wise. It was there that I was introduced to political correctness—not by my parents but by the community, including schools, community organizations, and the like. In their eyes, as a smart black kid, I could succeed only by understanding what to say, how to say it, and what not to say, and by making sure that I did not offend anyone. Of course, I would not seek to offend anyone; that is simply called having manners. However, how would I discuss and understand different points of view without knowing what those views are? I may not agree with a person's views on a topic. However, he or she has the right to have those opinions. More important, I was born on the island of Grenada, where political

23

correctness was never part of the discussion on any issue. We are a plain-spoken people who believe in saying what's on our mind without regard for what people think we should say. It is this kind of plain talk that allows us to understand where people are coming from without regard to anything else. Reflecting on those days in Florida, had I not had the guidance of a strong mother and father, I too would have ended up as a politically correct hack who simply would have been a sheep heading to slaughter.

I have offered an overview of my experience and so now will define for you what I mean by political correctness. I prefer a simple definition:

> *po·lit·i·cal cor·rect·ness*
>
> *pə'lidəkəl kə'rek(t)nəs*
>
> *(noun) the avoidance, often considered as taken to extremes, of forms of expression or action that are perceived to exclude, marginalize, or insult groups of people who are socially disadvantaged or discriminated against.*[1]

In this chapter I will explore how political correctness affects us in the social arena, in the political arena, and most importantly, on college and university campuses.

The Diversity Industry

A big part of political correctness is what is uncritically referred to as diversity.

This term is used most in the social arena. It has gathered scorn from many from across America, primarily because many see it as a

---

[1] https://www.google.com/search?client=safari&rls=en&q=political+correctness&ie=UTF-8&oe=UTF-8

"politically correct" way of preferring racial minorities over whites. And this is where the politically correct wheels fall off the wagon. Liberals have hijacked a term that was meant to represent the strength of the American fabric and weaponized it. And, given their arrogance, they expect the rest of America to accept it and get in line. They are quick to mock those who do not and to paint them with the scarlet letter "R" for racist. For those who are in racial minority groups and have rejected the political correctness of the left, liberals are all too happy to label them as Toms, sellouts, coons, and so on.

Liberals have installed a slave mentality across a wide swath of the population. In the actual days of slavery, slaves were controlled by whips, chains, and dogs. Liberals have learned well from that model. They simply have replaced it with political correctness, creating guilt and self-hate among minorities who do not subscribe to their message, and naming and shaming those who have dared to buck the system they put in place. The ghost of Boss Hogg has returned to haunt America's soul. Today's politicians would put Jefferson Davis to shame with their corrupt behavior.

Rather than address head-on the weapon of political correctness that they created, liberals immediately attacked conservatives who dared questioned their edict of diversity. It is indeed unfortunate that we live in an America where we have to divide ourselves by attaching a liberal or conservative label. The reality is that diversity backlash is a direct result of a liberal agenda that is designed to sow the seeds of strife. This is not to suggest that conservatives understand everything there is to understand about being in the minority. The fact is that neither do liberals. The reality is that the division began as soon as liberals began to weaponize the term "diversity" and dared anyone to question their right to do so. Diversity training is one of the most costly and popular "solutions" to bias if you believe leftist dogma. The fact is that there is no empirical data that backs up their claim that diversity training is as effective as they say it is. Yet, corporations and the government continue to spend millions of dollars on it. The question with diversity training is that it is designed to fail since much of it is designed to train people how to be politically correct.

Liberals so co-opted the term that in fact many thought it was just another word for "affirmative action," a term that so many resented and rejected.

To be sure, I am one of the premier thought leaders and a proponent of diversity as long as it includes everyone, with their similarities and differences.

In fact, I conducted original research on the competencies of the chief diversity officer at Cornell University, and as a member of the faculty at the time, I created the first program at an academic institution to certify professionals in diversity.

The certification was based on research and the desire to counter the profit-driven division propagated by the poverty pimps and race hustlers. Also, many corporations and organizations had begun to invest heavily in diversity, and I wanted to be sure that their efforts were sound from both a research and a practice standpoint.

By no means was I teaching people to be politically correct. That would have been an exercise in futility. Instead, my goal was to educate people that when we discuss and act upon diversity, we should realize that we have more in common than the politically correct chattering class would have us believe. In my view, the issue was understanding that diversity means everyone and that whites should not be excluded from the discussion.

When liberals moved toward diversity training, their need to weaponize the term "diversity" was out in the open for everyone to see, and it was not pretty. During that time, there was a widely accepted method of diversity training used by the now-defunct People's Institute, based in New Orleans. The course was entitled Undoing Racism.

In that course, people of all racial, gender, and ethnic identities spent a weekend together during which they were confronted literally about their racist ways. The "trainers," many of whom had no education or formal training in education, would go into a "classroom," where they would physically get up in the faces of the participants and tell them that racism was the fault of all white people. They measured success, in my experience, by the number of whites who cried at these sessions. Any nonwhite participants who dared challenge this practice were told that they were sellouts, and that accepting any white person as nonracist would mean the end of their lives.

Folks, this was the start of diversity training as we know it today, and the wounds remain open ones. Political correctness and the hijacking of the "diversity" term lie squarely in the hands of white liberal elites. This political correctness paved the way for the entry and acceptance of race hustlers and poverty pimps.

The People's Institute not only exploited division and political correctness, it aided and abetted a culture of racism in which everything is seen through a racial lens. The people conducting this "diversity training" realized, as the slave masters had, that there is profit in division. While they preached against slavery, as any decent human being would, they also instilled in many a mentality that would continue to enslave them for generations to come. The drama of getting into white people's faces changed nothing. Instead, like so much of the doctrine of political correctness, it sowed the seeds of discord that we are now reaping.

Poverty pimps are those who traffic in poverty for profit, with minimal if any expectations for change. Race hustlers, working hand in hand with the poverty pimps, sensed a golden opportunity. Many people were feeling a sense of white guilt, which the pimps and hustlers were all too happy to exploit.

Enter Race Hustlers and Poverty Pimps

As an independent thinker, I needed to know why I was being told that persons such as the Reverend Jesse Jackson, the Reverend Al Sharpton, Tavis Smiley, and Dr. Cornel West should be considered my role models. I was also told that Maxine Waters spoke her mind and that I should pay close attention to her, because her only motivation was the uplifting of communities of color. Being that I was told that, I immediately rejected it. First, I looked to my hard-working parents as role models. When I was a kid, my dad worked and my mom stayed at home and raised me, my brothers, and my sisters. This meant that she cooked, cleaned, and did homework with us. My dad always made sure that we set the table properly for dinner and that dinner was a family experience. There were no exceptions. My mom did not go to work until my siblings and I were of age, and even then, she and my dad were always home for family dinner. They never thought we were owed anything. My dad would always say, "You eat what you kill." In my view, they are role models. I don't idolize celebrities or sports figures, because I see them for what they do: a job. I do not believe that politicians or so-called race savers are role models, either. Too many of them are crooks, thieves, and self-serving arrogant clowns whose only motivations are power, money, and control.

Political correctness welcomed race hustlers and poverty pimps, with the single mission to drive division and destroy the reality of diversity. These people came in different versions. The original ones were Al Sharpton and Jesse Jackson—the fundamental shakedown artists at the time. Let me provide a brief background on each of these men so that you will be able to follow my logic about poverty pimps and race hustlers.

The civil rights movement in America was led in large part by the black male clergy. The reality is that while black women crafted the messages and strategies, the men took all of the credit. Regardless of that fact, blacks looked largely to the church and its leadership to help guide and lead them. This is no surprise, given that throughout slavery, the church and religion are what helped all blacks during the slavery period. Jessie Jackson burst onto the scene in a big way.

As an undergraduate, he was deeply immersed in the modern-day civil rights movement. Blacks and liberal whites began to notice him, particularly for his work with Dr. Martin Luther King Jr. Many recalled his march in 1965 in Selma, Alabama, alongside King. This event helped to catapult him to prominence and fame in civil rights circles. He used this as his entrance ticket to the race-hustling racket.

In the 1980s, he became a leading national spokesman for African-Americans. He was later appointed special envoy to Africa, and in 2000 he was awarded the Presidential Medal of Freedom. But there is another side of Jackson that was encouraged and revered by the political correctness movement. Elite white liberals had already declared themselves the savior of all but marginalized whites. But they did not want to be the ones out front doing the saving. They needed a patron whom they could support. That patron had to be black and male, so the marginalized community they had worked so hard to create would accept him. Jackson entered stage right. Fresh from his work with the much-celebrated Dr. King, he was ready for race hustling. Jackson would gather in churches and other community gathering places, where he would find out what the issues were.

He and his white liberal counterparts latched on to corporations as target number one, for many reasons. First, corporations had money; second, corporations were run by white men, and it was easy to create the corporate villain. Third, corporations played along. Whenever racial issues would arise, they would call on Jackson to "solve" them. The problem of course was that Jackson could not solve corporate racial problems. Corporations had to solve them. However, neither

Jackson nor corporations had any genuine interest in resolution. If they did, the problems would not keep happening. The corporations wanted the problems to vanish from the media spotlight, where the need for political correctness was a staple of American culture. Jackson wanted to make money regardless of the outcome.

There is no evidence that Jackson ever turned down a corporation as long as it paid him. A natural corollary of this was that if a corporation did not agree to pay his price, he would demand payments under the threat of a very public boycott, and so many did pay him as a result. For him, there was profit in peddling racial narratives, and corporations agreed. But what discernible changes were made in the lives of the people in the groups that Jackson was out to "help"? No statically significant data regarding outcomes is available on this. While Jackson made lots of money as a race hustler and poverty pimp, ironically, he fell out of favor when the first black president, Barack Obama, was elected. Jackson did not fall out of favor for his race hustling. Instead, he fell out of favor for his comments made on a hot mic. He said that Obama's nuts should be placed in a vise grip. Of course, there was a bit of sour grapes there. Despite his alliance with liberal whites, Jackson had not won his quest to become the first black president.

Jackson's demise cleared the way for the likes of Al Sharpton. Sharpton worked the streets of Harlem in his trademark velour sweat suits. A classic street brawler, Sharpton would chant slogans such as "No justice, no peace" while marching alongside his devoted crowd of supporters. Like Jackson, he too profited from division and political correctness. He exploited fake news to claim that Tawana Brawley, a teenager from Wappingers Falls, New York, had been raped by white police officers and, despite evidence to the contrary, continues that lie even today. Apparently, this fake news was not enough to disqualify him from being paid a reported seven-figure-plus salary as the host of a once-a-week show, on which his biggest challenge is reading the teleprompter.

My critics will say that I am against the poverty pimps' making money (and of course they will object to the label "poverty pimps."). My objection has nothing to do with their making money. It has to do with the following: besides being black, what qualifies them to do this work? And why aren't they transparent about what they do? What success have they had in changing organizations? These are all reasonable questions. However, I won't hold my breath for answers. The fact is that poverty pimps thrive on keeping their followers in poverty. They have no interest in getting them out of poverty. To do so would mean an end to their meal tickets. Poverty pimps subscribe to the notion that handouts and not a hand up are the way to success. But it is more than just that.

Poverty pimps and their allies on the left sustain the politically correct nonsense that eats at America's soul. Al Sharpton never saw an opportunity to race-bait that he did not like. For him, every issue involving black and brown people is a carefully presented stage play in which blacks are discriminated against, their "rights" to things such as Medicaid are trampled on by the white man, and on and on. I know of what I speak—as the owner of a pharmacy, I have people coming in with Medicaid, and even though some of their benefits are not covered, they demand something because Medicaid "owes" it to them. My pharmacy is not an arm of Medicaid. It is a business; it is not meant to lose money. I make that very clear to them. The politically correct culture in which we find ourselves would have me give something to them because they have a "right" to it. Breaking news: the government owes you nothing.

I can already hear my critics painting me as being anti-entitlement. Let me be clear, these benefits are meant as a way of helping others who are infirm and have no other means of getting benefits. Like any other benefits, they have limits and restrictions. They are not meant to be a way of life and passed down from generation to generation.

Even though poverty pimps and race hustlers know this, they are fundamentally afraid that if their followers are lifted out of poverty and then begin to think for themselves, they will then be able to clearly articulate and act upon the reality that the color of their skin is not what they bring to diversity. I have always said, "Do not ask me to do anything simply because I am black. Ask me to do something because I am capable of doing it." The poverty pimps and many organizations are coconspirators before, during, and after the fact in an America whose soul and blood are littered with political correctness, all so the poverty pimps can gain from division.

My article "The Ten Reasons Why Diversity Initiatives Fail"[2] was published to both praise and derision.

The derision was based on my conclusion that including whites in any discussion is crucial. Critics claimed that I was pandering to white men to gain acceptance. Let me address this directly. First, I pander to no one to gain acceptance. My work speaks for itself. Second, unlike so many who are beholden to the far left, my mom and dad blessed me with the ability to listen to the facts and then make my own decisions. This gift will last forever. Finally, I answer only to God and not to my critics.

In addition to the poverty pimps I mentioned, I will now explain how the original intent of diversity has gotten twisted. We have a long and storied history in America of affirmative action. When the original policies are read properly, it's clear that the purpose of affirmative action was to take steps to remedy past discrimination, address present discrimination, and prevent future discrimination. Just as people choose to ignore the framers' intent and plain language when looking at the Constitution, so does the politically correct chattering class ignore the original intent of affirmative action. The fact is that affirmative

---

[2] "Ten Reasons Why Diversity Initiatives Fail," Christopher J. Metzler, *The Diversity Factor*, Spring 2003, http://www.gsworkplace.lbl.gov/DocumentArchive/DiversityReferences/The%20 Diversity%20Factor.pdf

action was always designed to be a temporary measure and never to marginalize or punish whites. But in a politically correct America, the message, intent, and outcomes are dictated by the culture warriors who profit from division.

Any company or organization wanting to do business with the federal government has to submit a plan to explain how it would do so. Those wishing to do business also are required to do a utilization analysis with hard numbers explaining how this would be achieved. Let me distinguish between quotas and affirmative action. A quota is a fixed number that specifies the number of women, racial minorities, people with disabilities, and the like who have to be hired. Quotas are now and have always been illegal. Affirmative action and quotas, though often confused, are not the same thing. Given the agenda-driven propensity of the federal government, the concepts were muddled and set off a divisive firestorm in the public and political spheres. Many of the people in federal government wrongfully interpreted and practiced exclusionary tactics, which further divided the country.

It's a sign of how divided we are as a country that we cannot even agree on the nature of our divisions. Political correctness is such a part of American culture that we have done more than sink into partisanship; we are on the cliffs of destruction. Our political correctness culture has led to an over-hyphenated culture. We are no longer simply Americans. We are African-Americans, Chinese-Americans, White-Americans, and the list goes on and on. No wonder America's soul is so wounded.

How Political Correctness Shaped the 2016 Election

The 2016 election was an outright rejection of political correctness.

So that we avoid all speculation, just because one rejects political correctness does not make one a racist—despite liberal propaganda to the contrary. Many Americans had simply had enough of being told they could no longer be simply Americans. The country did some solid soul-searching and exhaled. Donald Trump was able to masterfully scrub and decipher the issues that many Americans cared about both domestically and abroad. He searched the depths of America's soul and was able to use political precision to lay bare the harm that political correctness had brought to the country. Although many thought it impossible that he would emerge victorious, they underestimated broadly the power of political correctness to wound the soul. Trump's election also exposed the reality that both the Democratic and Republican parties have been so obsessed with their own need for power, they have refused to address the cancer of political correctness that has become a staple of American culture. The reality is that he alone had the courage to address the issue head-on and without apology.

Liberals and their allies have worked tirelessly over the years to reshape American culture by weaponizing political correctness. Methodically, they used a completely misinformed and deliberately condescending definition of "diversity" to con us into believing that white men had had their turn and that it was now time for the "marginalized" people to take over. At Columbia University, I studied critical race theory so that I could understand its origins and its purpose. Simply put, critical race theory holds that race is part of original sin and cannot be addressed until white men give up power. The fundamental problem with this theory is that it seems that, as Americans, we are never to forget that race will always benefit whites and disenfranchise other "marginalized" groups, such as African-Americans, women, Hispanics, LGBTQs, and MENAs (Middle Easterners and North Africans). Because of a professed respect for "church and state," Christians are not to be considered.

This paints a much clearer picture to me as to why political correctness drove the 2016 election and its outcome. Liberals pander to their created marginalized communities strictly in an attempt to retain power and control. They have wrongfully interpreted the meanings of "diversity" and "affirmative action." But those communities are to blame as well, because they never critically looked at the issues, nor did they explore how political correctness simply was not in their own self-interest. As a fundamental matter, liberals have an agenda to level the playing field. But what does that mean?

The reality is that liberals are not advocating for a fair process—that's not enough, they argue. What is fair, so many of them say, is a fair outcome. But fair to whom? Let me translate: the vexing problem with political correctness is that liberals will consider an outcome fair only if it's an outcome they want, not the outcome the process decides is fair.

This hits me as fundamentally destructive to our republic. Political correctness and the policies that it spawns by design see America through the exclusive lenses of the oppressed and the oppressor. Followed to its logical conclusion, this means that by virtue of our race, we are born into one group or another, and the stigma of the oppressed and the oppressor will continue unabated. In liberals' view, the physical shackles of slavery have been removed; however, the effects of slavery remain. What they fail to acknowledge is that they are benefitting from keeping the oppressed in chains. By saying that affirmative action requires the hiring of people because of the color of their skin, for example, they are making people believe that political correctness underpins our culture.

They view the country as a rich mosaic of victimized groups that have been and continue to be exploited, stigmatized, and marginalized in countless overt and subtle ways. Liberals have perverted American history and branded it as a linear process. In their view, we should learn from American history that slavery was bad, that America has yet to atone for the sin of slavery, and that there will be success only when America is represented by race, class, and sex in exact proportions. This is laughable. How would you then represent people of multiple races and classes? Is this all that American history has taught us?

History teaches us and acknowledges that at the start of our republic, the spoils went to the victors. In our history, they were rich, privileged, Christian, straight white males who were also free. History also teaches us that as our country progressed, this changed considerably. America continues to expand rather than take away from the rights of all. It is this progress that history teaches us we should seek. Liberals are touting the message that we are supposed to become inclusive by being divided into our own demographic groups. Liberals, you see, have rebranded segregation as inclusion. In other words, political correctness is the segregation of our time. We are separate but equal until the white man gives up power or we take it. "Jump Jim Crow"!

Liberals would have us believe that they are much more inclusive than conservatives. But the research proves otherwise: "Not only are conservatives unfairly maligned as more prejudiced than liberals, but religious fundamentalists are to some degree unfairly maligned as more prejudiced than atheists."[3]

How Liberals Corrupted Diversity

The words "diversity" and "inclusion" have become deeply troubling, not for the words themselves but for what they mean in action. With political correctness as a weapon, non-minorities are included in diversity and inclusion—but only for the purpose of burning them at the stake. Elitist academics have branded whites' response to diversity as "white fragility." According to the term's creator,

"White people in North America live in a social environment that protects and insulates them from race-based stress. This insulated environment of racial protection builds white expectations for racial

---

[3] "People both high and low on religious fundamentalism are prejudiced toward dissimilar groups," Mark J. Brandt and Daryl R. Tongeren, *Journal of Personality and Social Psychology*, Jan. 2017, http://psycnet.apa.org/record/2015-49839-001

comfort while at the same time lowering the ability to tolerate racial stress, leading to what I refer to as White Fragility. White Fragility is a state in which even a minimum amount of racial stress becomes intolerable, triggering a range of defensive moves. These moves include the outward display of emotions such as anger, fear, and guilt, and behaviors such as argumentation, silence, and leaving the stress-inducing situation. These behaviors, in turn, function to reinstate white racial equilibrium.[4]

As an academic and researcher, the term strikes me as pandering, anti-intellectual, and downright stupid. It is the reason so many have rejected political correctness and liberal ideology. We have found ourselves divided because liberal ideology and political correctness now have forced us to pit the traditionally advantaged against the traditionally disadvantaged. That is, because white males in the past have traditionally been advantaged, they must pay for the sins of their fathers or be painted with the scarlet letter. Liberal logic suggests this is the solution. Thinking people disagree. We understand that pitting groups against one another leads to more division, not solutions. Also, political correctness encourages black men in particular to believe that they are victims. Victimology is not a solution or a cure; it is a cancer. Those who wish to use victimology as a crutch will soon discover that victimology looks backward and keeps them in the past. Victimology plus political correctness equals defeat.

The Academy

As a product of such intellectually challenging institutions as Columbia University and Oxford University, as well as having been on the faculties of Cornell University, Georgetown University, the City University

---

[4] "White Fragility," Robin DiAngelo, *International Journal of Critical Pedagogy*, https://libjournal.uncg.edu/ijcp/article/viewFile/249/116, Vol. 3 (3), 2011

of New York Graduate Center, and other institutions, I value learning and growing. I must admit that I had a somewhat romanticized vision of what it would be like to be a student at these storied academies. I also thought about what teaching at an institution such as Georgetown would be like. After all, Georgetown is the storied institution on the hill in Washington, D.C., with sweeping views of Potomac and where intellectual freedom flows freely. (NOT!) When I taught at that institution and served as a senior administrator there, my dreams were shattered.

When I joined Georgetown, my first dean was amazing. A thoughtful and innovative leader, he is a rarity in academic circles. For him, it was about academics and teaching and learning. Political correctness and anti-intellectualism played no part in the equation. At the time, I appeared as a political commentator, primarily on Fox News. I was a staple on both Bill O'Reilly's show and Larry Kudlow's show on CNBC. The Office of Communications at Georgetown gave the dean flak about my appearances. He stressed academic freedom. You see, the communications office felt I was articulating nonpolitically correct speech that was not welcomed. Imagine the liberal double standard. The university advocates for academic freedom. However, that advocacy ends when conservative academics express views. Liberalism is an ideology that works only when and how liberals say it does. Conservatives by nature are excluded, because they abhor indoctrinating people in political correctness. In liberals' views, this is their fight. We are not foot soldiers and "down for the cause."

The irony of it all was that I had liberal colleagues who appeared frequently on MSNBC but were not castigated. For example, Dr. Michael Eric Dyson was a frequent guest on many of the shows and was rumored to get his own shown on the network. Dr. Dyson is one who widely criticizes conservatives and praises liberals. But, the university P.R. Director did not see this as a problem.

When my first dean left Georgetown, the interim dean carried the mantle and directed the communications office to focus on the good I was doing for education. Georgetown made a decision to bring in a new dean. Some of my colleagues grumbled that she had been selected because of her gender. I did not engage in the dialogue. What I did realize immediately upon meeting her was that she and I would clash and that the time was right for me to move out of the academy. She immediately attacked me as being non-inclusive because I told staff that if they could not do their jobs, then I did not need them there; she found this to be unacceptable behavior. Yet, several high-level and highly talent people left because of her inability to lead.

What was unacceptable was her inability to appreciate that I am not and never will be politically correct.

It was her intention to fire me because I did not kowtow to her and the fact that I was never politically correct. As a conservative on a liberal campus, I did not belong. Never one to be caught with my pants down, I resigned before she could do so. It was perhaps the most liberating decision I could have made.

Georgetown University in my experience is not concerned about diversity. They are concerned about being politically correct. On the issue of race, the university has never gotten over its white guilt. In D.C., Georgetown was known by many to be a white, liberal elite school built on the backs of slaves. This is a P.R. issue that their diversity and affirmative action efforts were aimed to address this ongoing P.R. nightmare. Like many institutions at the time, Jesuit priests sold slaves to save Georgetown University from financial ruin, a group of descendants sued and called for restitution. So, diversity of thought or inclusion has never been on their minds. The Diversity Office is led by the university's long term Affirmative Action Director who lives by the mantle that her job is to attract "qualified" diverse candidates to campus. In other words, people who looked different than white men.

39

This phrase always makes me laugh and shows the twisted logic of liberals. We can conclude that the university would not hire unqualified people. So, why would liberals use that term to describe persons of the racial and ethnic diversity it was trying to hire all in a claim of "diversity?"

I was released from a trap where, despite stellar evaluations, praise from the university in its Dean's Report,[5] praise from students and parents, and exceptional peer reviews, I was targeted because of my refusal to follow a philosophy that I never have and never will believe in.

Always on my side, the Great Lord above said to me, "Son, you have much to offer; the time is now."

Georgetown is but a footnote in my career, and I have blossomed since leaving there. But how many conservative scholars are being excluded because they refuse to toe the politically correct line?

The rise of a conservative backlash on college and university campuses directly shows how many students are not being educated by brilliant minds but are being indoctrinated by closed minds. Political correctness is not simply academic, it affects us all. We have to be mindful that many liberal academic institutions have an impact on the future of generations to come, and that unless we insert ourselves into this morass, much will be lost. The idea is to teach people to think for themselves and make their own decisions. Political correctness is a danger to the republic. Don't say I didn't warn you.

William F. Buckley was a great guider of conservative thought. He guided us well on framing the question and reality of political correctness when we posted the real but provocative question of whether he would "sooner live in a society governed by the first two thousand names in the Boston telephone directory than in a society governed by the two thousand faculty members of Harvard University." Ronald

---

[5] https://static.scs.georgetown.edu/upload/kb_upload/file/Dean%27sReport_March2012-SinglePgs.pdf

Reagan denounced those who would trust "a little intellectual elite in a far-distant capital" to "plan our lives for us better than we can plan them ourselves." These wise patriots predicted where we are today on college campuses. I have been a college administrator and so understand the need to protect speech on college campuses. We find ourselves in a place not of protecting speech on many campuses but of overregulating to the disadvantage of conservatives. Colleges have become huge fans of implementing written speech codes and have a penchant for "tolerating" free speech only in certain geographically limited "free speech zones." A study by the Foundation for Individual Rights in Education found that one in ten schools have policies limiting free speech to small or out-of-the-way areas on campus.

The reality is that on many college campuses, the heckler, the one who shuts down free speech, is blessed and highly favored, while free speech dies a painful death.

The University of California, Berkeley was reportedly forced to spend more than six hundred thousand dollars and to have an overwhelming police presence simply to prove that the mob was not in control of the campus. The school offered advance "counseling" to any students or faculty whose "sense of safety or belonging" would be in great danger because the bogeyman was coming to the campus. The bogeyman was none other than Ben Shapiro—a thirty-three-year-old Harvard-trained lawyer who has been frequently targeted by anti-Semites for his Jewish faith and who vigorously condemns hate speech on both the left and right. Free speech won, and Shapiro spoke to many.

There were no riots and no reported safety issues.

The Federalists against the anti-Federalists, Abraham Lincoln against Stephen Douglas, Dr. Martin Luther King Junior against George Wallace. At so many times in our history as a people, it was speech—and still more speech—that led Americans to a more just, more perfect union.

But FDR saw it coming: "the forgotten men and women of this country," and a ruling class defined neither by its party affiliation nor by its wealth but by its grip on power, contempt for the American people, and globalist ideology. This is what will continue to ail America.

Aristotle, Machiavelli, and James Madison all taught us that politics is primarily a clash of interests. Ideas, it is true, shape interests—and vice versa, of course—but once they enter the public square, ideas must attach themselves to interests.

In Warsaw, President Trump identified the "fundamental question of our time" as being "whether the West has the will to survive."

For us Americans, the fundamental question of our time is whether our will to survive and replace the political correctness that has now overtaken mainstream America is strong enough. I am afraid it is not. First, far too many of us have ceded ground to liberals on this issue. Rather than engage in fact-based discussions, we have allowed ourselves to be silenced for fear of being labeled racists. When are we going to fight back with facts? We need to accept that for liberals, the "racist" label has no expiration date. As long as we play along, the more ground we cede. Second, this is a fight for America's soul. So when are we going to link arms, thoughts, and minds? While we live in different parts of a vast America, we are Americans for whom the republic is crucial. So we need to reach across those barriers that have kept us apart in our search for sustainable solutions. Third, we cannot expect, nor should we expect, the government to solve this for us. It simply won't happen.

CHAPTER 3

Fake News, Fake Facts:
Truth Is a Casualty of War
in Today's America

The news media is an American institution. I begin this chapter with an overview of the Pentagon Papers, because I am putting the current state of the media in context. Ultimately, the contents of the Pentagon Papers were not that interesting. In fact, the work was no page-turner. The Pentagon Papers were about the role of the press in challenging the role of government. In those days, reporters reported the news; they were not the news. The papers sparked an epic battle and a great confrontation over whether the press could override government's objections to their release. This was a time when journalists sought the truth and reported facts. that to today, when members of the leftist media spend a lot of time reporting on

Trump's tweets and hate speech, and colluding with leftist ideologues to present what they think is news. The journalistic era of the Pentagon Papers was an era in which facts came first and we did not need CNN to defend any ghastly excuse for reporting by airing a silly, juvenile commercial about an apple and bananas. It was not a period of mind control.

So, while the facts of the Pentagon Papers are dry, their history is rich and is missing from today's faux journalism.

Americans hold dearly freedom of the press and the First Amendment. The press has always been an integral part of the First Amendment. In fact, we have relied on the press to conduct investigations such as Watergate, the Pentagon Papers, and Whitewater.

How the Pentagon Papers Changed the Media

The official name of what has become known as the Pentagon Papers is the "Report of the Office of the Secretary of Defense Vietnam Task Force." It was secretly commissioned by then defense secretary Robert McNamara and ended up being a comprehensive history of American involvement in Vietnam from the end of World War II through 1967, more than ten years into the Vietnam War.

According to *The New York Times*, the documents reveal that "the Johnson Administration had systematically lied, not only to the public but also to Congress, about a subject of transcendent national interest and significance."[1] Among the bombshells within the report are that the U.S., led at the time by President John F. Kennedy, played an active role in the 1963 overthrow and assassination of President Ngo Dinh Diem of South Vietnam. Further, the papers reveal that the bombing campaign in North Vietnam was not deterring fighters, even though

---

[1] "Lessons from the Pentagon Papers," R. W. Apple, *The New York Times*, June 23, 1996.

the government told the American people that it was, in fact, dissuading fighters from joining the effort.

"The guarding of military and diplomatic secrets at the expense of informed representative government provides no real security for our Republic," Justice Hugo Black wrote in his opinion on the case of *New York Times Co. v. United States*, which made it legal for the *Times* and the *Washington Post* to publish the Pentagon Papers—which were classified at the time—without being censored or punished by the U.S. government.

"'They established the understanding you could publish anything you could lay your hands on and no one could stop you,' said Marcus Brauchli, former executive editor of the *Washington Post* and managing editor of the *Wall Street Journal*."[2]

What the Pentagon Papers reveal is that journalists back then did what has become known as "investigative journalism," and we the people could decide the truth for ourselves.

How the News Media Has Changed

In the past, we believed that journalists would investigate a situation and present the facts to us, and then we would make our own decisions. We traditionally did not rely on the press to tell us what to think. We always believed we were smart enough to make our own decisions and not be led by the nose by journalists. We now consume opinions and seek out outlets that fundamentally confirm the opinions we already have. I attribute this to several sociopolitical realities (which I discuss in detail in this book):

---

[2] "Did the Pentagon Papers matter?" Dana Priest, *Columbia Journalism Review*, Spring 2016, https://www.cjr.org/the_feature/did_the_pentagon_papers_matter.php

- The rise of a deeply divided America where truth is collateral damage
- A public education system that neither teaches nor rewards free thought, but instead penalizes free thought and expression
- The rise of liberal elite professors on college and university campuses all across the country, resulting in a fierce conservative backlash
- The rise of media personalities posing as journalists
- A twenty-four-hour news cycle driven by ratings, not facts
- The rise of corporate media giants, resulting in a need for a return on investment for shareholders regardless of quality
- The media's desire to see news more as reality TV and less as being about information.

When President Trump started using the term "fake news," many in the legacy media rebelled, accusing the president of attacking the media and undermining the fourth estate. I laughed and shook my head at the arrogance of an industry that prides itself on elitism and disdain for those who are not from the chattering class—an industry whose self-importance is littered with self-inflicted wounds. The reality is that many of those in the media are perched on a ladder and look down on the rest of us, who they believe should "eat cake." In their view, we are mere serfs who don't understand how things work and thus they should tell us. Our job is to follow.

Bullshit.

Our job is to call out the members of the media by any means necessary for what they have become. In fact, I believe we should expect that what we get in the legacy media is opinion, lies, lies, and damn lies. As such, it is time that we turn away from the legacy media or, at the very least, consider that so much of what it tells us is simply not true. Like so much of what is wrong with institutional America, the members of the media by and large have decided that their view of America is the only view that counts and that the rest of America should simply fall in line. I, for one, do not accept this, and I urge all Americans to reject this outright.

We Live in a Deeply Divided America Where Truth Is Collateral Damage

Let's look at a few examples:

CNN Has Become a Hangout for Celebrities, Not True Journalists

When Ted Turner started CNN, he brought the idea of news that Americans and the world could learn from. When he sold it, he sold it to agenda-driven partisans who turned the network into their version of the facts. The agenda was driven by a cult of personality. At CNN, the issues and truth were hijacked by highly left-leaning pundits and commentators who told the rest of America—through pandering rather than reporting—that we were simply too ignorant to take a set of facts and decide what they meant, so they would do it for us. CNN is no longer a news outlet, it is a cult-of-personality hangout, where the anchors and hosts sit high atop a proverbial ladder and look down on the rest of us as they tell us what is and is not normal and how we are to behave according to their definition of "normal."

One has only to look at the daily lineup of anchors and hosts on CNN. Anderson Cooper is not only an anchor at CNN, he is also a correspondent for *60 Minutes* (the once stalwart but now vanquished news program). He also hosts News Year's Eve celebrations and celebrity events and is seen on the red carpet, and we are supposed to believe that he brings us the news?

News in the era of CNN is a blend of entertainment, drama, and shouting. In a laughable attempt to shore up what it soon came to realize was its "credibility," CNN started airing a commercial it called "An Apple Is Still an Apple." In this rather amateur commercial, the network attempts to mock President Trump by indicating that his use of the term "fake news" to describe its reporting is a lie and that for CNN, facts matter. However, the reality is that the only facts that matter to CNN are the "facts" that it decides matter.

CNN is not a news outlet; it is a gossip outlet, with cult-of-personality figures playing journalists on TV. It traffics in dividing and separating because, like the Democratic Party, CNN knows that dividing America sells. CNN complains relentlessly about the president's tweets, but instead of simply reporting the news, it presents those tweets as "breaking news" every time.

The president has taken to Twitter to talk directly to the people. Members of the legacy media are livid that they have been left out of the conversation, so they are on the attack. We can thank the legacy media for the election of the president they love to hate but whose every word they are so obsessed with. Elections have consequences, and so does being swayed by the legacy media. We must wake up to this reality.

The View: Opinions, Not Facts

CNN is not the only guilty party here. Take Whoopi Goldberg and Joy Behar of The View. According to ABC, "The View is ABC Daytime's morning chat fest, featuring Whoopi Goldberg, Joy Behar, Paula Faris, Sara Haines, Sunny Hostin, and Meghan McCain discussing the most exciting events of the day. Hot topics in the news, the best experts in their field, celebrity interviews, and general entertainment are all part of The View, now in its 21st season on ABC."[3]

---

[3] "Fox News' Abby Huntsman Expected to Join THE VIEW," TV News Desk, *Broadway World*, August 10, 2018, https://www.broadwayworld.com/bwwtv/article/Fox-News-Abby-Huntsman -Expected-to-Join-THE-VIEW-20180810>

Let's be clear: despite ABC's longevity in media, this show is simply about opinions masquerading as facts. On any given day, the ladies of *The View* attack the president of the United States and/or the vice president with wanton abandon. They have the right to do so. However, never accept this as facts. Because it is their left-leaning *opinions.*

Fox News

Fox News has also had some less-than-factual encounters when reporting facts. One report stemmed from what the president said regarding the canceled visit of the Eagles football team to the White House. Rather than investigate for itself, the network relied on unreliable information.

Christopher Wallace of Fox News in a statement to *USA Today* said,

> *"During our report about President Trump canceling the Philadelphia Eagles trip to the White House to celebrate their Super Bowl win, we showed unrelated footage of players kneeling in prayer.... To clarify, no members of the team knelt in protest during the national anthem throughout regular or post-season last year. We apologize for the error."[4]*

Fox, at least, admitted its error.

* * * * *

America is a vast and complex country. The complexities are not too hard for us to understand. Yet far too many of us rely blindly on the media outlets of our choice either to reinforce what we believe or because we have bought into the cult of personality that is the news media. The fundamental problem with this is that by choosing to do

---

[4] "Fox News Apologizes after Eagles' Zach Ertz Blasts National Anthem 'Propaganda,'" Tom Schad, *USA Today Sports*, June 5, 2018

so, we are becoming a country where elites tell us what to do and too many of us accept it.

Some of us have begun fighting back. Many who voted for President Trump did so in part because they believed that the legacy media is among the biggest threats to the truth. We have become sick and tired of the opinion-based media, in which truth is a casualty of war. That war is a war for us to follow the path that the media tells us is the path.

I am reminded of what Thomas Jefferson had to say on this subject:

> *"Nothing can now be believed which is seen in a newspaper. Truth itself becomes suspicious by being put into that polluted vehicle. The real extent of this state of misinformation is known only to those who are in situations to confront facts within their knowledge with the lies of the day."*[5]

We Are in a Twenty-Four-Hour News Cycle Driven by Ratings, Not Facts

The issue of the press and democracy is not new. As Thomas Jefferson said, in a letter to his friend Edward Carrington in January 1787:

> *"The basis of our governments being the opinion of the people, the very first object should be to keep that right; and were it left to me to decide whether we should have a government without newspapers or newspapers without a government, I should not hesitate a moment to prefer the latter. But I should mean that every man should receive those papers & be capable of reading them."*[6]

Aside from the dated reference to newspapers, which was the media method of the time, Jefferson was spot-on. This twenty-four-hour

---

[5] Thomas Jefferson to John Norvell, Document 29 on Amendment I (Speech and Press), June 14, 1807, http://press-pubs.uchicago.edu/founders/documents/amendI_speechs29.html

[6] "Jefferson Quotes & Family Letters," Monticello.org, http://tjrs.monticello.org/letter/1289

news cycle poses a threat to democracy. In an interview with CNN, I said that the network wasted too much airtime on silly distractions and conjecture. The anchor's response was along the lines of, "Hey, we have twenty-four hours to fill."[7]

In the twenty-four-hour news cycle, every man is not able to understand why the news stations keep repeating the same thing over and over, why facts have become weaponized, and why the legacy media intends for us to be bystanders and follow blindly in the world it has set up. And so democracy suffers. As Jefferson implied, every man can't read the newspapers.

Our search for objectivity in the twenty-four-hour news cycle is futile. We ought to accept the fact that today's media is not objective because we don't demand it. Instead, we go along with it. If objectivity is so important to us, then why do we tolerate the existence of the objectively challenged institution that is the American media? The notion that market forces are supposed to dictate objectivity is simply wrong in the twenty-four-hour news cycle. The cycle is often driven by our comfort zones, who we like, how far the outlet takes our agenda, and not much else. For some of us, the American media survives, despite its dismal ratings, because the anchors and personalities confirm our basest and vilest proclivities. For others, we are bystanders to democracy and so don't take an active step in holding media responsible. For still others, the talk coming out of the twenty-four-hour news cycle is all talk and is in no way related to democracy.

Too many of us preach change but are simply too lazy to do the work that will lead to change. Moreover, if there were change, would we even know how to react to it?

The twenty-four-hour news cycle has been able to chip away at democracy because we have allowed it to. We would rather throw

---

[7] http://drchristophermetzler.com

stones than demand change. We are so divided that there is room for the twenty-four-hour news cycle to drive us into our camps where division breathes contempt, where no one is accountable, and lies become reality, while democracy dies a slow and painful death with us as accomplices before, during, and after the act—and we are fine with that. We are susceptible to propaganda now more than ever before, and no, it is not Trump's fault. It is our own fault.

The News Media Is Now Controlled by Corporate Giants

The news is controlled by corporate media giants, resulting in a need for a return on investment for shareholders regardless of quality.

In 1983, fifty different companies owned 90 percent of American media. Yet by 2011, only six companies owned that same 90 percent share of the media: Comcast, News Corp., Disney, Viacom, Time Warner, and CBS. So what does this mean?

We already know that there is no objective media anymore, so let's not pretend there is. We live in an era when corporate institutions tell us what to think and how to think about it, and many of us simply obey. The agenda of the members of the media is to appeal to their base, distort the facts, control the message, and control our minds. We have accepted this, and so we have no one to blame but ourselves.

News Is More About Reality TV and Less About Information

Just look at any news outlet. The "news" is not news; it is gossip. *Is there a difference between reality TV and the news?* No. On reality TV, one finds drama, betrayal, and lies. Corporate interests know this sells, so they set up the news to sell the same way. The anchors, reporters, and others feign outrage, are often loud and wrong, and have turned what was once journalism into Kabuki theater. Thus, the president hit a nerve by his use of the term "fake news."

So What Exactly Is Fake News? And Why Should We Care?

Too much of American news is fake news in which opinion rules, truth and facts are casualties of war, and down is up and up is down. The result is that too many in the American news media—the anchors and reporters as well as the know-nothing analysts are complicit in creating fake news. They willing participate in creating it because it benefits their interests. The key to sustain fake news is to have the consumers of fake news believe whatever the purveyors of fake news wants them to.

The legacy media is fraught with a sense of entitlement, a desire to both control and define the narrative, and an arrogance that is based on us versus them. The anchors know more than everyone else on so many subjects (at least that's what they want us to believe). They gather at the White House Correspondents' Association dinner, all dressed up to hobnob on the red carpet and bask in self-adoration and self-congratulation. Then they go back to work and try to pretend they report the facts.

Too many in the American media have yet to meet a fake "fact" they didn't like. Theirs is an alternate reality in which they create the narrative, critique the narrative, take credit for the narrative, and play the victim when they are called out for their daily steady diet of half-truths served cold. Yet they wonder why they are considered fake. The old saying "to the victor go the spoils" has never been truer than in the fake media. Those in the fake media are victorious over the spoils of American democracy.

Majority say fake news has left Americans confused about basic facts

% of U.S. adults who say completely made-up news has caused ___ about the basic facts of current events

A great deal of confusion	Some confusion	Not much / no confusion
64%	24	11

Source: Survey conducted Dec. 1-4, 2016.
"Many Americans Believe Fake News Is Sowing Confusion"

PEW RESEARCH CENTER

Source: *"Many Americans Believe Fake News Is Sowing Confusion," by Michael Barthel, Amy Mitchell, and Jesse Holcomb, December 15, 2016.*[8]

Fake News is not simply a slogan. We live it every date. The graphics below show that fake news causes confusion. That much is obvious. The issue though is not simply that it causes confusion. It is that we have to be able to recognize it and stop consuming it from those who peddle it.

In this chapter, I will focus on misleading content and manipulated content. The fact is that all democracies face the threat of uninformed citizens. America is no different. In fact, it seems that, over the years, the American public has become less informed and more susceptible to misleading "news." According to Massachusetts Institute of Technology researchers:

"A false story is much more likely to go viral than a real story.... A false story reaches 1,500 people six times quicker, on average, than a true story does. And while false stories outperform the truth on

---

[8] "Many Americans Believe Fake News Is Sowing Confusion," Michael Barthel, Amy Mitchell and Jesse Holcomb, Pew Research Center, Dec. 15, 2016, http://www.journalism.org /2016/12/15/many-americans-believe-fake-news-is-sowing-confusion/

every subject—including business, terrorism and war, science and technology, and entertainment—fake news about politics regularly does best."[9]

The legacy media, as a matter of course, traffics in misleading stories. The producers, anchors, and bookers decide on a story, create the narrative, and then get guests to validate it. They then depend on the American public to buy it: they sell those purchases (that is, ratings) to advertisers, who then get the public to buy their products, and the corporate giants are fed. Just another day killing democracy with the consent of too much of the American public. When accused of manipulation, people like CNN's Don Lemon offer the refrain "we are just doing our job." Kanye West came out in support of President Trump and Don Lemon went bonkers. He, who often accuses the President of using race to divide America used race to divide America. He hosted a segment with CNN's talking class of Bakari Sellers and Tara Setmayer mocked Kanye.

"Kanye West is what happens when Negroes don't read," Mr. Sellers said. Ms. Setmayer said: "He's all of a sudden now the model spokesperson. He's the token Negro of the Trump administration?" During the segment, Lemon laughed with glee. It was clear what he was doing, because Kanye who is black supports Trump and chooses to think for himself, his black card was revoked by Lemon. Lemon proves his point that he is just doing his job. He is right, since his job has become manipulating news content and using race to divide America. It is he who decides who is black enough. #FAKENEWS

The next chart is an illustration of the world in which we live. The reality is that information and disinformation are an integral part of our collective discourse. We live in an America where our collective

---

[9] "The Grim Conclusions of the Largest-Ever Study of Fake News," Robinson Meyer, *The Atlantic*, March 8, 2018, https://www.theatlantic.com/technology/archive/2018/03/largest-study-ever-fake-news-mit-twitter/555104/

Pew asked the experts for their insights on what's next for information in the age of "fake news." Five major themes emerged:
Many respondents believed that basic human nature will prevent improvement in the information environment.
Others suggested technology will create hurdles to improving the misinformation problem at scale.
Those who predicted improvement believe that advances in technology will help users better judge and filter misinformation.
Others said people will adjust to the environment and improve it in the long run.
Some respondents favor funding and supporting efforts to produce accurate information and expand information literacy.

Source: The Future of Truth and Misinformation Online," by Janna Anderson, published by Pew Research Center, Oct. 19, 2017.[10]

reality is based on political gamesmanship supported by the need to misinform. Power is not power without control of messaging, message definition, and message manipulation. Too many of us have given fake news the power to undermine the public while we sit by as passive consumers. Pathetic.

Many anchors are simply empty suits and comedic clowns who read from teleprompters. Despite all off his time on MSNBC, The Rev. Al. Sharpton still finds it difficult to read the teleprompter. They are unlike Walter Cronkite, the anchor of *CBS Evening News* from 1962 to 1981. Cronkite had the trust of the American people because his approach was to present all sides of any issue he was reporting on. This is not to say that he did not have his own political opinions. He did. He simply did not get in the way of his reporting the news.

To be sure, his approach was what journalism was supposed to be. He knew that facts mattered, and he was there to present them. He was not a showboat or a media provocateur. He was a journalist who covered some of the most history-defining and life-changing events of the

---

[10] "The Future of Truth and Misinformation Online," Janna Anderson, Pew Research Center, Oct. 19, 2017, http://www.pewinternet.org/2017/10/19/the-future-of-truth-and-misinformation -online/

republic, including the assassination of John F. Kennedy, the Vietnam War, the moon landings, Watergate, and the Egyptian-Israeli peace accord—which he himself helped broker by bringing the two nations' leaders together on one of his evening newscasts and eliciting commitments that they would meet each other face-to-face for the first time.

In contrast, today's news is anchored by headline-grabbing, attention-grabbing, self-important elites whose job is to shape public opinion without regard to consequences. This is among the many reasons why Americans are moving away from legacy media and moving toward different modalities to get their news. Most of the legacy media have lost the trust that the American people once placed in journalism and Walter Cronkite. Instead, we live in an era when we see the legacy media members as the cause of the problem because it is in their best interests to be that. Deep divisions and pandering are not the exception to the rule, they are the rule. The members of the media do not challenge division, they embrace division.

A Deeply Divided America

To be sure, America has always had its divisions—over slavery, race, Confederate monuments, the rights of gays, the role of women, and on and on. However, as a country, respect was the thread that held us together and stopped us from the division that now eats at our soul. Over the past ten years, I have noticed a seismic shift from respect to open hostility. Noticing that shift, the media has swooped down on our divided souls, like maggots crawling. Many of the members of the media have created an industry for unaccountable "experts" on their shows. The role is that of a contributor. From that perch, one gets to give one's unvarnished opinions about a topic on which he or she is an "expert." In the interest of full disclosure, I have appeared on many networks and have never been in the role of contributor, so I know of what I speak.

Here is how this works. The expert is pitched to the bookers and producers, usually by a public relations agent. If the network likes the expert, he or she is invited back. The expert cozies up to the producers and other decision makers—sometimes by being a constant presence—in the hope of getting a contract. The contracts can be lucrative. Contributors are paid thousands of dollars (some earn six figures) for contributing to the show. The danger of using contributors is that they often "contribute" on topics they have no idea about.

Take the case of President Trump and the Robert Mueller investigation. I have noticed that several contributors on CNN and MSNBC have said, "I am not a lawyer," but then have opined on legal jeopardy, collusion, money laundering, and fraud. Thanks for the disclaimer. So why do they spout their opinions?

The contributor culture is more about division and less about knowledge, and thus validates the very essence of fake news. Have we Americans gotten to the point where we depend heavily on the opinions of elites to help us decide who we are and what we believe? I am afraid that many of us have.

Look carefully at the résumés of these contributors. Do they speak for you? Have they experienced what you have? Do they get who you are? Have they ever been where you are? Most likely not. So why do you believe them? What are they contributing to? What's their value? When will we reject opinions being passed off as facts? What will it take for us to save the republic from the contributor storm? Have we become such a passive culture that facts are secondary to war?

Democrats are selling a message that protecting the "rights" of those who have entered this country illegally trumps protecting the rights of those of us who are here legally. I am an immigrant who entered this country lawfully. During that time, one had to prove that one would not be a burden to the United States, that one would uphold American values, that one would speak and write English frequently, and that one would put country first. Contributors constantly argue that we should have borders that are porous. This permissive philosophy is a threat to what it means to be an American.

According to their arguments, speaking English can be viewed as an insult to immigrants' cultures. My view is that if it is an insult to their cultures, then they should avoid that insult by staying in their respective countries. Contributors who argue otherwise are contributing to the destruction of the foundation of America as a nation. We welcome immigrants: that's fundamental to America. We are also a nation of laws that must be respected and followed. Immigrating to the United States is not a right; it is a privilege, and that privilege requires that we honor and respect it.

The question for we the American people is, what are the contributors contributing? The media has taken advantage of the deep division in America by selecting contributors on the left and the right to keep the division going. Is this what we Americans want? The media thinks we do, and not only will it give that to us, but it will profit from it.

The problem is that this cynical and Machiavellian tactic does nothing for journalism. It does, however, provide further division and distorts facts and reality in the media's quest to define and control the narrative.

The deep division stems not only from the rise of the fake-contributor class. It also stems from the networks' proclivity to produce shows that are unabashedly about division. I am a businessman and understand the nature of business. However, I also will not engage in any business that contributes to the erasure of fundamental principles of democracy. The contributor class in America does just that. It is composed of a bunch of hopeless, arrogant folks for whom ego and self-importance rule the day. Their feigned sense of self-importance is what sustains them.

The media's daily diet of disinformation and manipulation on issues such as immigration has driven many Americans to the breaking point. It also explains the rise in popularity of social media platforms on which we Americans are starting to take back the narrative that we have ceded to an increasingly elite, out-of-touch, and condescending media.

However, flocking to social media has its own perils and creates its own dangers to democracy. A 2017 study by researchers at New York University and Stanford on the impact of social media concluded (among other things) that

> *"Social media plays a bigger role in bringing people to fake news sites than it plays in bringing them to real news sites. More than 40 percent of visits to 65 fake news sites come from social media, compared to around 10 percent of visits to 690 top US news sites.*
>
> *Another study suggests that Facebook is a major conduit for this news. The more people use Facebook, the more fake news they consume, found Princeton's Andrew Guess, Dartmouth University's Brendan Nyhan, and the University of Exeter's Jason Reifler."* [11]

Called before Congress to testify on Facebook's propensity to encourage fake news, CEO Mark Zuckerberg said,

> *"It's clear now that we didn't do enough to prevent these tools from being used for harm as well. That goes for fake news, foreign inter-ference in elections, and hate speech, as well as developers and data privacy. We didn't take a broad enough view of our respon-sibility, and that was a big mistake. It was my mistake, and I'm*

---

[11] "Did Fake News on Facebook Help Elect Trump? Here's What We Know," Danielle Kurtzleben, npr.org, April 11, 2018, https://www.npr.org/2018/04/11/601323233/6-facts-we-know-about-fake-news-in-the-2016-election

sorry. I started Facebook, I run it, and I'm responsible for what happens here."[12]

Can You Believe It? On Twitter, False Stories Are Shared More Widely Than True Ones

In the Facebook study, that site was "among the three previous sites visited by respondents in the prior 30 seconds for 22.1 percent of the articles from fake news websites" observed by the researchers in their web data. But Facebook was "one of the prior sites visited for only around 6 percent of real news articles."[13]

To be clear, I do not buy the disinformation dribble that the fake news published on Facebook had any discernible effect on the 2016 election. I do not buy it because the evidence simply does not bear it out. My point is about controlling our own messages and narratives, and that social media is not a cure for all that ails our democracy. We must self-regulate and insist on facts first. When sharing content from social media, we should consider the source and check the facts ourselves. This is the way to preserve our freedom of expression while creating the change we want and need in the context of information and information sharing.

The point is simple. Have we been so co-opted by the media that we are willing to use the same disinformation techniques it uses in the name of developing and pushing our own narratives and controlling our own messages? If we are, how then can we criticize the media? The answer is that we cannot and still maintain any self-respect.

---

[12] "Did Fake News on on Facebook Help Elect Trump? Here's What We Know," Danielle Kurtzleben, npr.org, April 11, 2018, https://www.npr.org/2018/04/11/601323233/6-facts-we-know-about-fake-news-in-the-2016-election

[13] "'Messing with the Enemy': U.S. Lacks Consistent Narrative to Counter Weaponized Information," *Democracy Digest*, April 11, 2018, https://www.demdigest.org/messing-enemy-democracies-respond-weaponized-information/

We should continue to value the First Amendment and behave in a way that demonstrates our love for it and all of its principles. It is the backbone of our country. We have a major problem with institutionalized media in America. This problem is its need to decide what America should be. It wishes to make America in its own image. While members of the institutionalized media have the right to believe whatever they want, we have the right to reject them. The media has gone from reporting the news to creating the news. It expects that we will consume what it creates. But how can we consume a fake reality? The question for us is, when we see what the media is peddling, do we see ourselves? How does this blend of celebrity culture and "news" serve us?

Consider, for instance, the way the media often turns to a constant drumbeat of criticizing President Trump in order to drive ratings and to push its notion of what a president should be and how he should behave. This technique often leads to a highly problematic and vitriolic shouting match with no solutions. It also seriously damages the media's ability to inform and present facts. Along these lines, this chapter is a critique of the current media approach because it speaks directly to the division we are living with every day in America. This critique offers global concerns about the media and how we get and consume news. The reality is that Americans must become much more interested in recognizing disinformation by the media and disinformation on social media platforms. Our democracy cannot and should not be taken for granted in the flood of information that we both create and consume.

We must ask ourselves what we expect from media and what we expect from ourselves. I consume what is casually called "news" every day. However, I don't consume it blindly. I do so with my eyes wide open. I use social media frequently, because it gives me the opportunity to interact with people who are like me and different from me. These interactions with people across all spectrums of life enrich my understanding of information.

Inasmuch as claiming disinformation and media control are a reality, it follows that we Americans understand the problem. What is not clear is whether we are willing to create solutions or simply want to throw stones. Consider, for example, our propensity to tune in to the channels that most reflect our beliefs. To be clear, there is nothing wrong with that. In fact, I believe that self-selection and choice are good things. But are we sending messages to the media that division sells while criticizing it for sowing division? I believe that the media is largely responsible for the division in the first place. That is, because the media provided divisive coverage, consumers sought alternatives—in the cable news space, for example, we ended up with two left-leaning channels (CNN and MSNBC) and one right-leaning channel (Fox News).

The long-term impact of the media's manipulation of truth is hard to predict. However, the evidence so far is jarring. We are a polarized, divisive, separate America. It is time that we Americans examine critically our relationship with media manipulation. We cannot allow the current system to tear us asunder. It is time that we isolate any media that undermines democracy and replace it with facts. We can decide for ourselves what the facts mean. Let's demand truth and not spin. Many journalists have conservative or liberal view. Why don't they simply reveal this rather than pretending that they are objective?

The media is controlled largely by corporate interests. We fund corporate interests. Let's de-fund them so that they understand that their lies, lies, and damn lies will no longer be tolerated. Our democracy depends on it.

CHAPTER 4

Same Color, Different Class: White Liberals and the Hillbilly Class

Growing up in America, I was constantly bombarded with messages from school and other places that white people had it made. To be white, I was told, was to be privileged. There were no poor white people anywhere. I was fortunate to have parents who told me never to believe everything I read or heard, to investigate things for myself. And I did.

What I found was that the use of language to divide people was commonplace in America, that some people felt comfortable using divisive language to explain the behaviors of people with whom they never came in contact, and that liberalism supported this approach.

Slavery: The Original Divide Between Black People and White People

Division by race, class, and gender is not uniquely American. There are many countries where division has been used as a way of gaining access to power and control. Perhaps one of the reasons that division in America rapidly became a way of life was because of America's experience with the complexity of slavery. I offer this as a reason, not as an excuse.

In slavery, there were issues of race, color, and class. It is no secret that for hundreds of years, the ruling power structure in the United States was controlled by rich, powerful, white, male landowners. In order to maintain their power and wealth, they had to have people work the land at little or no cost to the ruling power structure. The most readily available labor pool was made up of African slaves. The fact is that millions of those slaves worked the land with no reward for most of their lives. The beneficiary of their labor was the ruling power structure.

The word "slavery" is by no means just an American term; in fact, it comes from the Latin *sclava*, meaning "Slavonic captive," referring to the ninth-century slavery of Slavic people, but it came to mean anyone in captivity, not only Slavs. My point is a simple one: slavery provided the language of division not only because of its brutality but also because of the language its beneficiaries had to use to maintain control—the most infamous of which is "nigger." It was not only a word but also a way of controlling the way America saw the African slaves. Soon, whites, no matter their economic class, adopted it.

Divisions Among White People According to Class

The issues of division and stereotypes are not new. In the case of white liberals and working-class whites, the division issue has spawned an economic, political, and rancorous debate that only white liberals benefit from.

I learned very quickly that white "elite" liberals heap scorn on the white working class. Let me be clear: I use the term "white working class" not because I believe that it is a positive term but to illustrate the disdain that too many elitist white liberals have for the average white person in America. Make no mistake, white liberals have created class warfare, and the white working class has responded. One can easily see the revenge of the white working class, through its vociferous use of social media (Twitter in particular) to express curiosity and outright disdain for the people who by their choice of words and actions go out of their way to deride the white working class. In the social media postings of many working-class whites, one can see the snark as they expose their fascination with the ultra-wealthy and their mockery for the professional class. Given the physical separation of white liberals and working-class whites, disdain, mockery, and snark are served from a distance and are often reserved for cable TV pundits, celebrities, news anchors, and the like—those who profit from the swamp.

Watching White Do-gooders "Help" Poor Island Black People

Growing up in South Florida in the '70s, I had to learn for myself what it's like to be a liberal and have liberal beliefs. I had some experience with white liberals in Grenada, where I was born. Many whites on so-called pilgrimages came to the island to help the poor blacks in the country be better people. They felt that they meant well, so we should be grateful for their efforts. The same well-meaning people self-segregated in compounds with the most breathtaking views of the island and had maids and servants, whom they paid very little.

That experience has stayed with me as I hear the language and sound bites spoken by white liberals. I was a child at the time, so I had not yet developed the language to critique "white liberals," but I knew what they stood for, and I did not like it. They sought power, control, and a free hand to develop culture on their terms. They would shape the discussion to fit their wants and needs, and would support the underdog as long as they could control the underdog and that underdog had fidelity to them. They played nice but acted in the most vicious of ways to control the dialogue. Under the veneer of niceness was the reality of disdain.

What Exactly Is a White Liberal? What Do They Believe?

When identifying a white liberal, in my experience, there are several clues to consider. This is not to suggest that all white liberals are evil. It is to suggest that too many white liberals criticize conservatives and conservative policies without exploring their own intersection of race and class. The first is a persistent attitude of being arrogant, paternalistic, and basically insulting. It involves the acceptance of the idea that to behave like they do is normal—except they get to decide who can behave like they do and who is socially acceptable to include. This, of course, excludes poor and working-class whites. Too many white liberals have an enduring sense of supremacy, which one can see in their choice of language—for example, "deplorables," "poor white trash," "hillbilly," and so on. These words are not meant to be terms of endearment. They are meant to be an attempt to separate white liberals from the undesirable whites—especially the ones who voted for Donald Trump.

The problem here is that not only poor and working-class whites voted for Trump. Some very wealthy white people also voted for him. White liberals choose to ignore this, however, and instead single out the poor and working-class whites who voted against their self-interests. Of course, their sense of superiority and entitlement lets them decide what those self-interests are.

Yet white liberals wonder why poor and working-class whites have such disdain for them. They wonder, but frankly, in my opinion, they don't care. The only reason they now "care" is because they see the reality of that disdain and are now looking to shift blame onto poor and working-class whites; many white liberals believe that this group (which they have marginalized) is now using its power, to the chagrin of white liberals. A reasonable person would think that, given the shifting power dynamics, white liberals would seek ways of aligning with the group they have castigated. This simply will not happen. Instead, white liberals will attack the people they consider to be their enemy and continue to divide America. Because in their view, they can.

Next is the false sense of what is ideal. After all, liberals created idealism. Their idea of ideal is to accept the concept of the "civilizing mission" of white liberals. The logic goes something like this: poor and working-class whites do not suffer from biological deficits. But, in white liberals' view, that is not the issue. The issue is that poor whites suffer from an endemic inferiority in a culturally complex world. They must be stopped, lest they corrupt the culture.

Liberal whites believe that poor and working-class whites are culturally backward and terribly unsophisticated. Thus, the only hope for them is to be educated by white liberal elites who know best how the world works. Of course, for any group to have this view of another is unacceptable. In fact, it is vile, exclusive, and simply a display of hate and division that white elite liberals relish. The fact that they claim to be "liberal" and "inclusive" seems to come with this sort of assumption about their cultural superiority.

Their attitude toward poor and working-class whites is simply laughable. White liberal elites know that their attitudes toward poor and working-class whites are instinctually and practically dishonest. However, they maintain those attitudes and attack with force and vitriol anyway. This is because they take comfort in their level of isolating poor and working-class whites. White liberal elites need a way to separate themselves from the poor-white-trash inferior white people in Appalachia; it is this base and vile need that supports their sense of superiority. One can maintain superiority and unearned privilege only by attacking someone who is the enemy. This victor/enemy model works for white liberal elites.

But have they asked themselves how this stereotyping and abhorrent behavior is any different from the "nigger/coon/Sambo" model that was applied to blacks? Answer: it's not. White liberal superiority is grounded not in reason but in ego, power, and an uncomfortable relationship with truth and ethics. The problem is that liberal whites fundamentally believe they exist to help the poor and the downtrodden. Sounds good, but it is fundamentally flawed because they believe that, by the privilege of their whiteness, they set the rules. I have been in rooms with many who have praised my success and then said, "You have achieved all of this despite being black. There are still good white people out there." My response: Go kick rocks in your privileged rock gardens.

As to working-class whites, my experience has been that liberal white elites believe that they are the bald-headed stepchild. On the campaign trail with my great friend Kenyon, a proud working-class conservative stumping in Virginia, I watched how white liberal elites ignored him and questioned his education and his experience. It is as if he were Joe the Plumber or Hillbilly Joe. It is this kind of disdain that continues to divide America.

In their view of what it means to be a white liberal elite, a few things are necessary:

- An unmatched ability to wield power and influence, no matter how those things are obtained
- The belief that whiteness and liberalism make the world go round
- A lack of shame regarding the belief that white liberals alone have the ability to wield power, however that power is obtained
- The desire to do whatever it takes to keep that power

In their view, poor and working-class whites are the exception to whiteness and liberalism that shows exactly what is wrong with the body politic in America. The American body politic thrives on division to keep power. The truth is that for many poor and working-class whites, the refusal to be liberal is not a deficit, it demonstrates sophisticated taste and is worn as a badge of honor.

White liberals are fond of the term "othering," which means to consider someone as other than being normal or acceptable. Consider this, from an article titled "Saving Liberalism":

"Identifying the "other" is part of what binds a group together, by creating mental rules for identifying who is in—and who is out. Othering can be pretty harmless, even beneficial, when it builds community among, say, sports fans rooting against the New York Yankees or the Dallas Cowboys (which is why sports leagues hype artificial rivalries between teams).

When it comes to national identity, though, othering carries substantial risks. Policymakers seem to have vastly underestimated the need for othering—and its consequences. Sure, scholars always knew it existed and there has been some good research on it. But many did not recognize the extent to which othering was a central threat to liberalism and globalization, and even started to think that cosmopolitan integration was inevitable."[1]

---

[1] "Saving Liberalism: Why Tolerance and Equality Are Not Enough," Jeff Colgan, *Foreign Affairs*, Jan. 13, 2017, https://www.foreignaffairs.com/articles/2017-01-13/saving-liberalism

But hold on. The term "othering" was developed by white liberals and is commonly used by them to accuse other whites of making non-whites seem strange, foreign, and not normal. The "logic," however, does not apply to "othering" poor and working-class whites. White liberals get to decide how and when the term applies. As the ultimate arbiter of the use of the word and its application, only liberal whites have the upper hand. Poor and working-class whites be damned. Thus, when it comes to the so-called white working class, white liberal elites see nothing wrong with "othering" them. In fact, if white liberal elites are to be believed, all white working-class people are the same.

Jump Hillbilly...Jump

This is not a new issue. During the administration of President Lyndon B. Johnson, the term "hillbilly" was in vogue. Hillbilly logic gives white liberals the opportunity to distinguish themselves from what they see as the tragic white common man. In their view, hillbillies are akin to the blacks who live in the ghetto. In their view, the hillbilly is poor white trash, of whom white liberals are so ashamed. In their view, whiteness is a privilege that is reserved for the educated, the moneyed, and the posh. Thus, white liberals are free to look down on hillbillies with wanton abandon. Let's keep it real: it has been and still is socially acceptable to heap scorn on hillbillies (also known as white trash).

"Hillbilly" is not a foreign word to Americans and the world: its history goes back at least as far as the Gilded Age. In *Hillbilly: A Cultural History of an American Icon*, historian Anthony Harkins explains that "hillbilly" is just one of "dozens of similar labels…and ideological and graphic constructs of poor and working-class southern whites coined by middle- and upper-class commentators, northern and southern."[2]

---

[2] "Hillbilly Elitism" (a review of *Hillbilly Elegy*), Bob Hutton, *Jacobin Magazine*, Oct. 1, 2016, https://www.jacobinmag.com/2016/10/hillbilly-elegy-review-jd-vance-national-review-white-working-class-appalachia/

Many elite white liberals take great comfort in using the term, because it sets them apart from their brethren, who they believe are savages. The term "hillbilly" has a history based in Scotland. History teaches us that Scottish and Ulster-Scots (Scots-Irish) people, the Scottish Lowland and Ulster Presbyterians, came to the United States in massive numbers during the 1700s. They did not check their identities at the border. Instead, they came intact, with their traditional music. Since their patron was William, Prince of Orange (who defeated the Catholic King James II of the Stuart family at the Battle of the Boyne, Ireland, in 1690), these immigrants came with a certain loyalty to him and his traditions. In spite of that reality, once they were in America, they were widely considered to be savage country folk devoid of class, upbringing, and world savvy. For many white liberal elites, the "savages" represented a backward civilization. White liberals have normalized disdain toward America's "white trash."

The 2016 election brought this out into the open. Although there had already been much whispering about the "white trash" vote, it became pronounced in the 2016 election cycle. For liberals, it proved to be a strategic blunder and an epic fail.

Hillary Clinton: The Tragic White Liberal Elite

Hillary Clinton is the archetypal white liberal. As the tragic white liberal figure, she is a woman of liberal ideology who ignores the hardships of working-class whites. Her sense of entitlement reigns supreme.

Consider her words as the Democratic nominee for president: "You could put half of Trump's supporters into what I call the 'basket of deplorables'.... They're racist, sexist, homophobic, xenophobic— Islamophobic—you name it."[3] One can spin this any way one wishes. But I look strictly to the text of her speech.

[3] Hillary Clinton, in a speech given during the 2016 presidential election, Sept. 9, 2016, https://en.wikipedia.org/wiki/Basket_of_deplorables

Her statement showed how, for many white liberals and Democrats, attacking working-class whites is a calling card they are happy to use. The fact that doing so makes America even more divided is of no importance in the world in which they live. Although she, as well as other liberals and progressives, paint themselves as inclusive, their idea of inclusion excludes conservative whites and the "basket of deplorables." It also shows why so many working-class whites don't see themselves in the Democratic Party. White working-class people pass down their treatment and feeling of exclusion to future generations, as they should.

Clinton is the poster child for the white liberal elite. From her Ivy League education to her role as a lawyer at the Children's Defense Fund and a presidential candidate, she believes that poor whites are an embarrassment to her race and may even be traitors to her race. Consider her life's work. She was educated at Yale, was a partner at Rose Law Firm, was the First Lady of Arkansas and then of America. Dick and Debbie Salt of the Earth are foreign people to her. They are white and working class. She rejects them because of that. In typical white liberal elite fashion, she believes that one of the ways she could get and retain power is to marginalize working-class whites. For her, the price of victory is well worth dividing America and piercing its soul.

Moreover, working-class whites are not liberals, and in her view, they vote against their own self-interests by electing conservatives. The issue of poor and working-class whites voting against their self-interests has gained momentum and traction among liberal pundits, liberal academics, and Hillary Clinton. In liberal academic circles, there was a whisper campaign that the stupid poor and working-class whites would regret voting for Trump because he would make them poorer. As often happens with whisper campaigns in academia, whispers turn into research, research leads to publication, and then the topic goes to the public square. A series in *Politico* picked up the mantle and asked:

"Are working-class white voters shooting themselves in the foot by making common cause with a political movement that is fundamentally inimical to their economic self-interest? In exchange for policies like the new tax bill, which several nonpartisan analyses conclude will lower taxes on the wealthy and raise them for the working class, did they really just settle for a wall that will likely never be built, a rebel yell for Confederate monuments most of them will never visit, and the hollow validation of a disappearing world in which white was up and brown and black were down?"[4]

The White Working Class Fights Back

The *Politico* language further solidifies one of the reasons that poor and working-class whites reject mainstream media—it's because of the disdain with which the mainstream media speaks about them. For far too many poor and working-class whites, journalism by way of name-calling is something they have become used to. However, rather than retreating to a place of despair, they are fighting back and are highly motivated to do so. The election of President Trump is but one example of how they have begun to fight back.

The support for President Trump is real because these people have been marginalized and excluded by white liberals. The divisive politics of white liberals simply have blinded them to the reality of what was on the minds of white working-class voters in the 2016 election. Trump's election was a rejection of the status quo. The time had come when white working-class voters simply had had enough of the Democratic Party's exclusion and hypocrisy.

---

[4] "Does the White Working Class Really Vote Against Its Own Interests?" Joshua Zeitz, *Politico Magazine*, Dec. 31, 2017, https://www.politico.com/magazine/story/2017/12/31/trump-white-working-class-history-216200

To be sure, many white liberals disagree with me. In their view, members of the white working class who voted for Trump were not motivated by the need to reject the status quo. They were motivated by racial bias, and Trump knew that and took advantage of it. As one study of Trump voters concludes:

> *"In many ways, a sense of group threat is a much tougher oppo-nent than an economic downturn, because it is a psychological mindset.... Given current demographic trends within the U.S., minority influence will only increase with time, thus heightening this source of perceived status threat.'*
>
> *And don't think for a moment that this attitude was exclusively held by men. A second new study looks specifically at female Trump voters—and finds that, much like their male counterparts, they were largely driven by racial resentment and support of traditional gender roles."[5]*

The Pew Research Center (a left-leaning think tank) conducted what has been touted by many white liberals as a "definitive study" of the issue and concluded:

> *"Trump's margin among whites without a college degree is the largest among any candidate in exit polls since 1980. Two-thirds (67%) of non-college whites backed Trump, compared with just 28% who supported Clinton, resulting in a 39-point advantage for Trump among this group. In 2012 and 2008, non-college whites also preferred the Republican over the Democratic candidate but by less one-sided margins (61%–36% and 58%–40%, respectively)."[6]*

---

[5] "Research Finds that Racism, Sexism, and Status Fears Drove Trump Voters," Tom Jacobs, *Pacific Standard*, April 24, 2018, https://psmag.com/news/research-finds-that-racism-sexism -and-status-fears-drove-trump-voters

[6] "Behind Trump's Victory: Divisions by Race, Gender, Education," Alec Tyson and Shiva Maniam, Pew Research Center, Nov. 9, 2016, http://www.pewresearch.org/fact-tank/2016/11/09/ behind-trumps-victory-divisions-by-race-gender-education/

Is Race a Factor in Elections?

Is it possible that some voters are motivated by race when selecting a candidate? Recall how much black voters were motivated by voting for the first black president. To many black voters and liberal whites, this was an important and historical event. For many black voters, Obama could do no wrong.

In the 2016 election, we saw white working-class voters who were motivated by the candidate they thought most identified with shaking up the status quo. They asked themselves, "When did the status quo work for me? In 2008? Or in 2012?" The answer was neither. So, for them, this in and of itself was a historic moment—a moment in which many Trump voters believed that Washington was broken and could finally have someone who could fix it. So was race a motivating factor for all Trump voters? No more so than race was a factor in the election of Obama. Many liberal elite whites will dismiss that view as self-hating and delusional. I am used to that, so there is nothing to see here, folks.

I'm writing about this in the context of the presidential election because it is still on our minds and is the easiest-to-understand recent event. But contempt for what white liberals often call the "hillbilly crowd" is an everyday occurrence in America and contributes further to the division that hinders America's soul.

White liberal elites simply refuse to accept their role in the worsening division of America as they keep tearing away at its soul. They continue using their best efforts to put forth a witch's brew of classism mixed with stereotyping in an effort to keep America divided.

It's a badge of honor in certain liberal circles to laugh at the very real struggles of the poor. When a story of horrific racism comes across their feed, the Twitter wags ironically cluck about "economic anxiety," to mock the narrative that economic anxiety made that racist punch that black person or call in that bomb threat.

I have asked white liberal elites a simple question: In all of your wisdom and experience, have you ever found that promoting economic division is ultimately destructive to America's soul?

Their responses have been on several levels. First, they deny that they promote economic division. Instead, they say they are simply providing the facts. But what facts? That poor and working-class whites are inferior because they are poor and/or working class? I remind them that their "facts" are based on stereotypes that they use to maintain their own perception of superiority.

They scoff at me and say, "Why would you support the poor and/or working-class whites who have voted to keep you down by electing Donald Trump? Are you voting against your own self-interests?" Actually, I remind them, Donald Trump supports my economic and social mobility interests. In their view, those hillbillies and poor white trash are who overwhelmed the polls and gave us Donald Trump, a terribly ill-mannered savage of a man. In their view, they are simply trying to save the country, much like they did during slavery—when they helped the republic heal its soul by changing its arcane and stereotypical views of blacks. They ushered in the need to help black people by creating social programs that made them able to survive. Of course, they choose to omit the fact that many of these programs are handouts, not a hand up. I offer this context to show how liberal white elites' perception of themselves is continuing to divide America. In an effort to "help," they insult. They claim that they are saving America from becoming its most destructive self. I ask, who will save America from them?

Here is what is wrong with elite white liberals: they have taken the people they call white trash, crackers, and hillbillies to the breaking point. I am not talking about the election of Donald Trump. I am talking about the context in which we live daily. As a result of the persistent refrain of insults, those who are not from the urban areas are acting to take back control of their lives. They no longer wish to live in an alternate reality.

That alternate reality manifests itself most in the #resistance movement. The #resistance movement was born out of pure spite and unabated contempt for poor and working-class whites. White liberal elites have tried to cover up their naked contempt for the hillbilly crowd by joining with blacks, Latinos, and socialists. It is what I call the "basket of hate." Their cynical approach has been described in articles like "Democrats Hold Lessons on How to Talk to Real People." How much more cynical and condescending can one be? You are resisting the real people while trying to teach people how to talk to them? Why now?

The reality is that America is very diverse, and that diversity includes all people. White liberal elites don't define "diversity." The fact is that rural white people are an important part of the American fabric. Until Democrats, progressives, and socialists accept this, America will continue to be divided.

Hillbilly bashing is not new among liberals. The sideshow of liberals, progressives, and socialists working hard to out-disdain one another on the question of "hillbilly hate" is pathetic. Their petulant, self-aggrandizing vitriol lays bare their quest for power at all costs. White liberal elites refuse to learn that dismissing an entire part of America does nothing to help find America's soul.

They also need to understand that the hillbilly crowd is much more advanced and logical than they believe. Our democracy is representative, of course, as far as I know. They still have not learned that elections have consequences, and ignoring the people they have decided are the "other" is political suicide.

The good news for conservatives is that this behavior will buttress conservative support; it will not diminish it. Liberals, Democrats, and their allies have an uncanny ability to overplay their hands and will continue to do so in promoting a divided America. Conservatives are masters at turning anger into action. Recall the tea party and other rebellions. Democrats and their allies have an uncanny ability to whine, cry, and attack. They have created the mantra of inclusion as a way to show that they listen and care for all. Liberal whites, Democrats, and their allies have for years pounded America with political correctness as an "ideal" way of dealing with a complex agenda. They reap what they sow. Political correctness has come back to bite them in their proverbial behinds. Rather than accept that and deal with it, they have shifted the blame to poor and working-class whites. That dog don't hunt.

Despite all of Hillary Clinton's baggage, Democrats made her their presidential nominee. They have yet to apologize to the country or their party. She accused whites of being racist, yet her campaign for the nomination against Obama was heavily tinged with racism. Consider this statement (in 2008) by her chief strategist, Mark Penn, about Obama: "…[H]is roots to basic American values and culture are at best limited. I cannot imagine America electing a president during a time of war who is not at his center fundamentally American in his thinking and in his values…"[7]

And this advice from Penn to Hillary Clinton:

"Every speech should contain the line you were born in the middle of America to the middle class in the middle of the last century.… Let's explicitly own 'American' in our programs, the speeches and the values. He [Obama] doesn't."[8]

Democrats also knew that she did not think the people in rural America were of any value. In a CNBC interview, former Pennsylvania governor and former chair of the Democratic National Committee Ed

---

[7] "The Front-Runner's Fall," Joshua Green, *The Atlantic Magazine*, Sept. 2008, https://www.theatlantic.com/politics/archive/2008/08/penn-strategy-memo-march-19-2008/37952/

[8] Ibid.

Rendell admitted that the party knew she was not a candidate who could win against Trump and that her campaign had made a mistake by not courting the white working-class vote: "Of course, hindsight is 20/20. But if I was in charge of the campaign, I would have sent Hillary into those white working-class areas in Michigan, Wisconsin, and Pennsylvania."[9]

His admission proves the fundamental problems that the Democrats have with the white working class. They believe this class is a necessary evil. While Trump was addressing rural America, Clinton was addressing celebrity America. In her view, she did not need to engage rural America because she was not one of them. Her phrase "I'm with her" was in and of itself laughable for its arrogance. I have always thought that the candidate had to be with us, not we with them.

The Democratic Party owes America an apology for nominating HRC. She gained 21.6 million dollars by speaking to banks and other corporate groups after leaving the State Department. Yet she has the unmitigated gall to call people "deplorables" and immoral? Her condescending and profit-driven method of operation is among the reasons that the Democratic Party owes America an apology for subjecting us to such an arrogant, classist person.

She did little to help America become united and much to maintain division. This country is best when we have a two-party system that functions to serve us, the people. Unfortunately, Democrats and their allies resist rather than serve. And what has their resistance gotten them? It has gotten them nothing. In fact, it has backfired. Solving America's woes requires coming together on a host of topics and putting solutions over politics. White elite liberals refuse to accept this. They have chosen disdain and division above all else.

---

[9] "Clinton Campaign made a mistake, didn't heed warnings: Fmr. PA Gov. Ed Rendell," Michelle Fox, cnbc.com, Nov. 15, 2016, https://www.cnbc.com/2016/11/15/clinton-campaign-made-a-mistake-didnt-heed-warnings-fmr-pa-gov-ed-rendell.html

The fundamental problem with the Democratic Party is that it simply does not understand modern-day America. Its leadership is entrenched, it has no identifiable moral center, and it relies on tactics that are simply useless. For all of its preaching on diversity and inclusion, it has not adopted a modern voice on those subjects.

Had Democrats done so, they would have realized that white, rural, working-class, and poor people are not buying their feigned sense of inclusion. For their party, America's soul is of no moment. In fact, they gain more, they think, by the politics of division than by the politics of inclusion. They expect Americans to follow them as sheep to the slaughter.

Hillary Clinton wanted to make history as the first female president of the United States. She made history instead as one of the most arrogant, self-serving people ever to seek the presidency. The Democratic Party also made history as the most out-of-touch party in modern-day politics. There can never be an effective two-party system without people who come together to solve problems. America is a country rocked by division and the question of how to solve issues of inclusion, a country in which politicians have made a career of working in Congress because the benefits are too good to give up. Unless we the American people right that ship, white elite liberals will continue to wreak havoc on our collective lives. My critics will say I am being unfair to the Democratic Party and its allies because I do not acknowledge that since 2016, Democrats have reached out to the hillbilly crowd. Really? What was their motivation? The shellacking they got?

As University of California law professor Joan C. Williams writes:

"Hillary Clinton, by contrast [to Trump], epitomizes the dorky arrogance and smugness of the professional elite. The dorkiness: the pantsuits. The arrogance: the email server. The smugness: the basket of Deplorables. Worse, her mere presence rubs it in that even

women from her class can treat working-class men with disrespect. Look at how she condescends to Trump as unfit to hold the office of the presidency and dismisses his supporters as racist, sexist, homophobic, or xenophobic."[10]

Williams has hit the nail on the head. White entitled liberals refuse to engage with the working class. So for us to believe that there is now some sincerity in understanding the hillbilly caricature that they created to maintain power is laughable at best. If white liberal elites want to keep America's soul intact, they must come to the conversation open to listening and learning. The white working class and poor are generally not envious of success; in fact, many admire success. What they don't appreciate is the arrogance and disdain of people like Hillary Clinton.

White liberal elites have made a cottage industry of racism. As such, they are quick to dismiss as racism any disagreement with their liberal posturing. This outright dismissal without inquiry is a substantial roadblock to a united America. Few would argue with the tone and tenor of racism in the 2016 election. However, let's also be clear that Democrats had a strategy to expunge white working-class Trump voters from their party. And why would this be acceptable? It is not. On the issue of white liberal elites and white working-class voters, the Democratic Party has painted itself into a corner—a corner that isolates Americans based on snobbery and elitism. It is a corner that wields race in a way the Dixiecrats did. It is a strategy that relies on separation and the damning to hell of America's soul.

Have white liberal elites learned anything from history? Have they not seen and experienced the tearing asunder of our American soul and how that has led to war? Is it a race war that they want? Americans

---

[10] "What So Many People Don't Get About the U.S. Working Class," Joan C. Williams, *Harvard Business Review*, Nov. 10, 2016, https://hbr.org/2016/11/what-so-many-people-dont-get-about-the-u-s-working-class

value success; we also value the fundamental principles that our country was built on and that have kept the republic strong. I am deeply concerned that this separatist behavior that is now normal in American culture is the rule and not the exception. Racial and class attitudes span all races and classes. Yet white liberals seem oblivious to that. It is that superiority complex that turns off so many of the white working-class people in America. On the subjects of wealth and poverty, white liberal elites should recall that "there, but for the grace of God, go I."

CHAPTER 5

How the Swamp Is Undermining the Republic One Bite at a Time

As one who has spent a fair amount of time in Florida, I am accustomed to the stench of the Everglades and the many creatures that infest the swamp. The area is hot, it stinks, and evil oozes easily from swampy waters. While tourists tour the waters of the glades on airboats, the swamp dwellers scour the glades to determine what their next evil act will be. Swamps are evil places. There is but one mission for swamp dwellers: destroy the legitimate order of things in the swamp so that they can redefine that order. The swamp creatures have no soul, no center, and many exist for the sole purpose of surviving at all costs. There is a certain pungent smell from the swamp that, no matter how one tries, one cannot get rid of. While D.C., is not a swamp like the Everglades, it has similar qualities. First, it's very hot at times of the year, second it stinks of corruption, and third, lobbyists and politicians infest it. American citizens are like the tourists on the airboats, they tour D.C. like the tourists on the airboats in Florida (figuratively, not literally).

Swamp on Steroids: Washington, D.C.

I came to Washington, D.C., initially to study law at Howard University School of Law. Upon my arrival in D.C., I noticed that it was a different place.

Everybody would look around to see who was the most important person in the room, liberal values were central to the core of D.C., and nothing was as it seemed. As a young black conservative, I soon discovered that challenging the liberal status quo was the kiss of death for many. Marion Barry was king at the time, and he could do no wrong. Career politicians were in vogue, and America was on a steady decline into liberal chaos.

The swamp is nothing new in D.C.; people are only now starting to acknowledge it. The problem with the swamp state is that it has caused the country to spiral out of control into a radical and rabid partisan existence where ideology has replaced common sense. This would be fine if the ideologues simply affected their own little corner of the world. But, like the creatures in the Everglades swamp, they affect the entire United States.

Here are a few elements of the swamp:

- Unelected paper pushers who believe that they, not the elected officials, have the power to make and enforce laws.
- People who are in the same social circles are the "kingmakers" and decide who is in and who is out.
- D.C. is a social circle where who you know and how you can benefit them are all that counts.

- Many people are enemies in public and best friends in private.

- Lobbying is a mainstay of Washington. Elected officials make decisions based in part not on what is best for America, but on what is best for them now and in the future.

- For too many elected officials, D.C. is a long-term career. They either stay in office for a long time and enjoy the benefits or leave office and profit from the time they have spent in office.

- Meaningful legislation is rarely passed in Washington anymore.

- Washington creates a profile of what a president should look and behave like, and what he should decide.

- Any president who fails to adhere to that profile is destroyed in the press and in the public square.

The Capital of Corruption: Tales from the Hood

I spend a great deal of time in the swamp of D.C. and have become accustomed to the lavish parties at the homes of lobbyists and their friends. The more I attend, the more I realize how the vile and unmitigated quest for power is destructive to the republic. And the more I realize that it matters not who is POTUS but whom the swamp dwellers control. It is not life in the fast lane; it is life in the power lane.

As I stepped into one such party recently, I looked at the bevy of servers, impeccably dressed, serving lobster, crab, escargot, frog legs, and more on heaping platters. The party was supposed to be a birthday celebration for someone who hardly anyone outside of D.C. would know but whom swamp dwellers pay homage to. In the room were politicians from both sides of the aisle who knew full well not only that the birthday boy could make it rain, but that he could also stop their cash flow and kill their careers. I made small talk, courtesy of a top-shelf open bar, with several lobbyists who were big in the healthcare and immigration spaces. Many had pending legislation before many in the room, but they hardly mixed and mingled with members and their staffs. Ethics rules? What ethics rules?

What many outside D.C. fail to appreciate is that while members are important, so are their staffs. Congressional staff people are trusted advisers to their bosses, and they often help shape policy and legislation. They wield just as much power as elected officials, and those seeking access to power know this. Thus, while those seeking access to power may not get direct public access to members of Congress, they do have access to congressional staff, and so they achieve the same result. The lavish parties prove this without a doubt. They are events at which staff members are hounded and surrounded by rock stars, and they soak up each and every moment of it.

The swamp not only is filthy, it is an affront to our republic. The swamp's culture gladly allows for public servants (those we elect to office to look after our interests) to take money and fight against our interests. In the lavish party culture of Washington is where legislation actually gets done. The room of that event I attended was lined with staff members partying in the lap of luxury and with whom there were inappropriate interactions with special interest groups who were currying favor. When will we the people take back control? Or will we sit back and elect officials who will act against our own self-interests?

Corruption: Build It and They Will Come

Too many of us Americans forget what happened in the not too distant past and so act as if corruption, for example in D.C. is something new. Yes, the Murtha case was about 12 years ago but I use it for illustrative purposes and to encourage us that past is in fact prologue. Not too long ago, federal investigators raided the offices of the PMA Group, a venerable D.C. lobbying firm. The charge: alleged improper campaign contributions. PMA had a reputation for charging high fees while helping clients receive multimillion-dollar earmarks from congressional legislation. The firm's biggest cheerleader was Rep. John Murtha (D-PA), who enjoyed a high perch on the House Appropriations Committee. That perch came from one the same perks that unions have: seniority. In other words, his power was not based on the legislation he had passed or the number of significant things he had done for the country. It was based on pure, old-fashioned seniority. The longer you have been there, the more power you have. Competence, outcomes, and American policy are casualties of seniority.

Having been a member of Congress for more than three decades, Murtha was a champion of projects and largesse to his district in Western Pennsylvania. PMA founder Paul Magliocchetti once worked for Murtha on the House Defense Appropriations Subcommittee. According to Taxpayers for Common Sense, Murtha arranged thirty-eight million dollars in earmarks for PMA clients in the firm's executives and clients were among Murtha's biggest sources of campaign contributions.[1]

Another firm, defense contractor Kuchera Industries—located in Murtha's hometown of Johnstown, Pennsylvania—was also found to be involved in fraud a few years later. Kuchera received millions of dollars in defense contracts over the years and also had close ties to Murtha. This demonstrates the close and corrupt nature of politics.

---

[1] "Nonprofit Connects Murtha, Lobbyists: Ties to Pa. Group Mutually Beneficial," Jonathan Weisman, WashingtonPost.com, Dec. 25, 2006, https://www.washingtonpost.com/archive/politics/2006/12/25/nonprofit-connects-murtha-lobbyists-span-classbankheadties-to-pa-group-mutually-beneficialspan/af16286a-7304-46bd-b4d1-86149366a940/?utm_term=.df0eac2de4b5

But Murtha is just one example. Unfortunately, in the swamp, such corruption is the rule and not the exception. The Murtha case is critical to understanding why D.C. is such a corrupt place. First, it illustrates that claims by members of Congress to the contrary, they simply cannot and should not be regulating themselves. Second, after the case Congress passed a flurry of rules and regulations to stop corruption yet in 2018, corruption continued on both sides of the aisle. We the people claim that we are angry about corruption but we often don't see it as a major campaign issue. If you think that the Murtha case was an example of corruption, look no further than Paul Manafort.

* * * * *

Paul Manafort was indicted by the special counsel investigating President Trump on a number of charges involving corruption. The media and others rushed to link the president to Manafort, saying that since Manafort had served (albeit briefly) as Trump's campaign chair in 2016, his indictment was proof that the president was involved in collusion with Russia. Manafort lived and profited from the swamp long before working on the president's team. For nearly a decade, he was a dweller of the swamp in the Ukraine. His benefactor and single client was the president of Ukraine, Viktor Yanukovych. Manafort's job was to make sure that Yanukovych was elected and stayed in power so that, like a pig to the trough, he (Manafort) could eat.

He was assisted by his trusted minion and fellow swamp dweller Rick Gates, who pled guilty in the special counsel's probe. A frequent ladder climber and swamp creature, Gates once proudly proclaimed when speaking to his fellow robber barons, a group of Washington lobbyists, "You have to understand, we've been working in Ukraine a long time, and Paul has a whole separate shadow government structure.... In every ministry, he has a guy."[2]

Both Manafort and Gates are examples of why there is a need to not only drain the swamp but to blow it up with sticks of dynamite. Manafort joined the Trump campaign because he had something to contribute; he joined the campaign because he was broke and, like so many swamp dwellers, wanted to sell access for cash. He is a pimp and wanted to make the nation his hos. Yes, he worked for "free." But his "free" has cost the nation much.

The power helped fill Manafort's bank accounts: according to his recent indictment, he had tens of millions of dollars stashed in havens like Cyprus and the Grenadines. Regardless of whether he served as chairman of Trump's campaign or not, Manafort is still an example of why Washington and its politics of corruption are a threat to the republic. We the people cannot and will not put up with a culture where the swamp creatures get rich by using unearned power and influence. Politicians who continue to believe we are ignorant and that we give them permission to profit from that corruption because they bring money back to our districts should realize that the money they bring back is nothing compared with the money they earn as profit. Too many politicians have no soul: they have been overcome by avarice and greed. Manafort was convicted by a Virginia jury on 8 counts. Facing a trial in D.C., he pled guilty to avoid trial in D.C. Although Manafort was not a member of Congress, lobbying which is permitted and encouraged by Congress is a major part of the swamp that is choking the republic like the algae that is chocking the ecosystem in Florida. But, America, our feigned anger is not enough.

* * * * *

[2] "The Plot Against America," Franklin Foer, *The Atlantic*, March 2018, https://www.theatlantic.com/magazine/archive/2018/03-paul-manafort-american-hustler/550925

I have watched in utter disgust the rebranding of Congresswoman Maxine Waters. In liberal circles, she is being called the resister-in-chief for her relentless attacks against President Trump, branding him as corrupt. Recently, she was hit with a complaint from the Federal Election Commission alleging corruption. She has raised hundreds of thousands of dollars each election cycle from some of her state's biggest politicians paying to be listed on her slate mailers—sample ballots traditionally mailed out to about two hundred thousand voters in Los Angeles highlighting whom she supports. Since 2004, the campaign, in turn, reportedly has paid 750,000 dollars to the congresswoman's daughter, Karen Waters, or her public relations firm, Progressive Connections, for help producing those mailers. Yet Waters has lambasted Trump as one of the most corrupt politicians ever. In fact, after his inauguration in 2016, she called him a scumbag, immoral, indecent, and inhumane. She branded his staff the "Kremlin Klan."

But this is not about name-calling. It is about Maxine Waters, corrupt politician and swamp dweller who attempts to profit from her own corruption and from the liberal lapdogs who give her cover. While she has been granted near icon status by many of her sycophants, perceived conflicts of interest and nepotism prompted a liberal watchdog group, Citizens for Responsibility and Ethics in Washington, to include Waters on a list of corrupt members of Congress.

Swamp Dweller-in-Chief

To understand the role of corruption in her DNA, let's examine her role in a federal bailout for OneUnited Bank, on whose board her husband served and in which he had a sizable stake, during the 2008 banking crisis. Waters arranged a meeting with the Treasury Department, at which OneUnited representatives sought federal bailout money. The bank eventually received more than twelve million dollars from the Troubled Asset Relief Program.

That led to an ethics investigation into Waters's involvement in setting up the meeting. Investigators eventually concluded that she had disclosed her financial ties to the bank, recused herself from decisions involving it, and believed the Treasury meeting would involve representatives from minority-owned banks generally, not just OneUnited. The Ethics Committee found that she had not violated any rules barring the use of one's position for financial gain.

But that was not the case for Waters's then chief of staff, Mikael Moore, who also happens to be her grandson. Investigators found that Moore had taken actions "unambiguously intended to assist OneUnited specifically." He received an official reprimand. The fact that the committee found that Waters was not involved shows how the swamp works. Backroom deals, lavish parties, arm twisting, and quid pro quo are the culture of the swamp. In the swamp, back scratching and ass kissing rule the day. Underlying all of this is the fact that the committee did not want to be accused of sex and race discrimination, so boss Maxine was cleared and her grandson (her chief of staff) took the beating with a feather duster.

Waters said that Moore had not violated any rules, and that is true. House ethics rules designed to combat nepotism in the legislature prohibit members of Congress from hiring most family members. If Democrats take control of the House in 2018, Waters will be the chair of The Finance and Banking Committee. Once again, the fox will guard the henhouse.

The fact that there are "rules" to govern members' behavior is laughable. First, who writes the rules? The rules are written by the members themselves. Does anyone believe they will write rules that will punish them? The fact is that the "rules" are no rules at all. They are designed to make the American people believe that Congress does not need citizen oversight. They can police themselves.

Second, the fact that the committee decided that Moore did not break any rules is a huge corruption problem. It is necessary to read the plain text of the rules here. Grandchildren were not on the list of prohibited hires when Waters gave Moore the top post in her Washington office. But of course, liberals do not generally believe in strict construction; they prefer to ask what the meaning of "is" is.

In a Daily Beast interview, Waters shifted the blame to Trump, stating that she rejected any suggestion that her past run-ins with congressional ethics authorities and watchdog groups had any bearing on her Trump remarks. As if this were not outrageous enough, she who claims that she values transparency and the free press chided The Daily Beast for even asking her any questions about her ethics charges and suggested that they were an attempt to distract from what she saw as the real issue, Trump and his corruption:

> *"This story that you're trying to put together, to somehow make it look as if I am as bad as a Trump, and I do bad things, and that somehow I don't deserve to criticize him, is not credible.*
>
> *I'd like you to think about what you're doing and why you're doing it and I'd like you think about whether or not you're trying to maybe protect the president somewhat, cleanse him a little bit, make him look a bit better, to make it look as if other people don't have the right to point these things out about him and other people who you make it look as if they have the same kinds of problems."*

Presumably with a straight face she added, "I want you to think about that and think about whether or not this is a story you really want to do."[3]

---

[3] "Maxine Waters: Trump 'Lied Again,' I Didn't 'Call for Harm," www.thedailybeast.com, https://www.thedailybeast.com/waters-trump-lied-again-i-didnt-call-for-harm

Despite her outrageous claim and her love of self-dealing and corruption, Waters has been lionized by the left. Dubbed "Auntie Maxine" and being branded as the black woman who tells it as it is, to many on the left she can do no wrong. She is Helen of Troy. But if she tells it like it is, why doesn't she tell all of it? Why doesn't she tell about her life of corrupt politics? Why doesn't she tell that, for all of her time in Congress, her constituents are not significantly better off since she has been their representative? Attack her, and you are a racist and sexist. She has been able to successfully con her supporters into weaponizing race and gender to defend against her life of corruption.

Despite her clear record of abuse and corruption and the fact that Congresswoman Waters lives outside of the district she represents, those on the left are among her most ardent defenders. They defend her in part of her longevity in Congress and in part because she holds tremendous power on the Banking and Finance Committee. Plum committee assignment, entrenched member of congress and a thirst for influence is a lobbyist dream. Even with this knowledge, consider this dishonest and clearly partisan praise for the congresswoman; it only fans the flames of twisted logic and alternative facts:

"Congresswoman Waters (D-California) is one of the fiercest and most accomplished Congresspersons in the history of the United States Congress. She is a compatriot of former Congressman Bill Clay and now a colleague of Missouri's Congressman Lacy Clay. She is a tireless fighter and relentless leader and advocate for women, civil rights, labor rights, political, education and economic rights for all regardless of color, gender, nationality, creed or orientation. She has a brilliant and fearless record of public service, tackling difficult and controversial issues and combining strong legislative and public policy advocacy with fierce grassroots organizing.

Congresswoman Waters has been at the forefront of every major battle waged in the last 50 years to make this a better nation.

She stands tall and fights hard to protect the gains that our forefathers and mothers secured with their sweat, blood, tears and lives.[4]

CNN pundit Angela Rye was only too happy to jump on the defend-Waters bandwagon:

[Rye]: My point is very simple: I demand that people stop requiring Congresswoman Waters to behave in one way while everybody else can do something else. Nancy Pelosi said let's 'make America beautiful again.' Whose America is she talking about? Steve [Cortes], at the beginning of this program, said this isn't America, this is—what America are you talking about?

[Rapper]: Childish Gambino artfully told you what America is and what it looks like. Let's deal with the distinctions you all see, because some of us see a very different America.

The fact that [Senate Minority Leader] Chuck Schumer called what a black woman said un-American is problematic and this is the reason why Democrats have a hard time uniting the base.

[Erin Burnett]: But can he not say that just because of the color of her skin?

[Rye]: It has everything to do with the fact that this black woman is intimidating to some people who can't handle the truth. It has everything to do with race.[5]

Of course, Rye herself was executive director of the Congressional Black Caucus Foundation and knows Waters well. In fact, Rye herself cut her political chops by being closely aligned with Waters. The devil is in the details. Classic swamp politics.

---

[4] "In Defense of Congresswoman Maxine Waters," Walle Amusa, *St. Louis American*, June 26, 2018, http://www.stlamerican.com/news/columnists/guest_columnists/in-defense-of-congresswoman-maxine-waters/article_98a96940-7988-11e8-9f44-3f88bda671eb.html

[5] "Angela Rye: Maxine Waters Criticism Has Everything to Do with an Intimidating Black Woman Telling the Truth," RealClearPolitics.com, https://www.realclearpolitics.com/video/2018/06/26/angela_rye_maxine_waters_criticism_has_everything_to_do_with_an_intimidating_black_woman_telling_the_truth.html

And herein lies the problem: corruption knows no color, despite what the left would have you believe. Maxine Waters is corrupt, and those who support her reward her corruption. I could care less about her gender or skin color. I do not question her political savvy. What I do care about is the fact that if Democrats win the House, she would be chair of the House Banking and Finance Committee, where she would have unchecked power to unleash even more corruption on America.

* * * * *

A divided America survives and thrives on race baiting and corruption. It also requires supporters before, during, and after the fact. The swamp has all of that and more—thus the need to blow up the swamp and return government to the people. The swamp is run by a bunch of useful idiots and their merry men.

We Americans are to blame for allowing the swamp to not only survive but thrive. We are so disconnected from the swamp that we send our elected officials there without holding them accountable. We rely on the stale phrase "throw the bums out," but we re-elect the bums every chance we get. We elect a president and then expect him to drain the swamp. The swamp creatures come from our home districts, and we send them to office. We believe in so much the swamp dwellers say, without proof. We elect a president to disrupt the swamp but don't elect enough disruptors in Congress. Too many of us simply don't rely on our moral centers to do what is right for this country.

I have included three examples of swamp dwellers in this chapter to illustrate a point. That point is that corruption is the rule and not the exception in Washington, and unless we make deliberate change, it will only get worse.

We say we want the president to drain the swamp, but he cannot do that when we keep electing corrupt politicians and their staffs. The culture of corruption cannot be changed by one man alone. The republic has to take on this task. Too many of us throw stones but do nothing to help. We are happy to complain but do not vote; we call for change but believe that change is somebody else's job. We don't support a disrupter; instead, we criticize him, and we lay back and point fingers when it is too late to fix problems.

The Press: More Swamp Dwellers

Since the election of President Trump, he and the media have engaged in a war in which he has accused the media of being fake and they have accused him of being a liar, being unhinged, and destroying America. To be sure, the president is a provocateur, and that is, in part, why he was elected. The problem is that the media is using outmoded and highly inefficient tactics to duel with a master communicator and has settled into a safe space in which it is the victim. If the media was being real and not fake, they would acknowledge that they are in part responsible for his election. At first, they saw him as a joke, a jester, a buffon. Yet, every tweet he issued, they covered it. They covered it to show how, in their view, he was not fit to be President. Had they been true journalists, they would have discovered the anger that was a fever pitch in the country and that he spoke to it. Too much of the mainstream media chose ideology over news and then cried when Trump was elected President.

In fact, many have accused him of being mentally unstable and have stopped just short of calling him an idiot. Trump's quibble in part with the media is that they are swamp dwellers. That is, the members of the media in America are no longer reporters of facts; they are creators of acts. They are members of the Washington swamp.

I have been around politics, television and Washington for a long time. Serving as a political consultant, a T.V. commentator, and a

Washington insider. Based on this I am offering the reasons why the media is such fake news.

- The White House Correspondents' Association is an organization that spends much time in the same social circles unlike ordinary Americans.
- The White House Correspondents' Association's annual dinner has become less of a friendly roasting of the president and more of a leftist political attempt to embarrass any conservative president.
- The members of the press are more concerned about being celebrities and less concerned about facts and news.
- The press makes no distinction between facts and opinions.
- Too many Americans have decided to allow the media to tell them how and what to think.

The job of the press is to report news, not to make news. However, in this current climate, the press is more inclined to make news than report it. The notion that the president is an opponent of freedom of the press is an example of the press's creating news. What the president is an opponent of is a Washington-based press corps that is concerned more about scoops than facts.

Take a look at the major press outlets and examine how they cover the president. Their "reporting" always assumes that the president or his staff is lying. It is a presumption of dishonesty that infects their coverage.

Liberals decry the rise of the conservative press. What they don't understand is that the rise of the conservative press is a direct reaction to the proliferation of a liberal press that has an uncomfortable relationship with the truth. There is no evidence that the president wants to shut down the press or have state-run media. There is evidence that, as creatures of the swamp, the members of the liberal press are biased against the president because he does not fit the mold that they have helped develop of what a president should act like, behave like, and look like, and because he does not kowtow to them. This has, by and large, made them more Baghdad Bob and less Walter Cronkite.

It has also set up a testy and contentious relationship that distorts the facts and misinforms the public writ large. It is in part why so many are leaving mainstream media and turning to alternative platforms in the digital space. Washington creates a sense of entitlement with a sprinkle of delusions of grandeur that provides oxygen to the swamp. Power, control, and privilege are what most members of the swamp-dwelling Washington press corps thrive on. A civil society requires a solid press corps. It also requires a diligent one in which the issue is about facts and not the personalities of those in the press corps. Surely, the press should challenge any president. But that challenge should be an exchange based on facts, not speculation or supposition. The job of the press remains to inform the American people, not to draw conclusions for us.

America has earned great respect around the world for the relationship between the press and the government. That respect is beginning to erode, in part because what we witness daily is a resorting to opinion journalism. Sadly, opinion journalism is now most of American journalism and not merely a part of it. This approach has plunged American society further into division, with far too many Americans gravitating to networks that agree with their points of view. American journalism is no longer a marketplace of ideas. It is a marketplace of opinions supported by big corporations who traffic in division to gain profits.

Why the Swamp Is More Powerful Than Ever

At the core of swamp politics in Washington is the process by which elected officials make policy. That is, we send elected officials to Washington to come up with policies and legislation that will change our lives for the better. Of course, we don't—nor should we—elect policy experts to these positions. The swamp, with all of its unelected paper pushers, decides how policy is made in Washington.

It goes something like this: a congressman has a particular policy issue in mind. He presents it to his staff and asks for their advice. While he may have policy experts on his staff, his staff is generally limited in scope and size and has to focus on many policy issues, some of which may be contradictory. In addition, he cannot make policy by himself. His staff also reaches out to other members to get their support in moving the policy forward. The rule-making and policy-making process is a maze. It has been designed by the paper pushers and the lobbyists, and is often referred to by many as "job security." Given that the congressman is unable to navigate the process and its many pitfalls single-handedly, he is unable to ensure that there is no insider takeover and manipulation. Thus, he turns to the paper pushers and lobbyists for help. In the swamp culture, the lobbyists deploy their expert research teams and work with think tanks to provide research that cannot be provided by the congressman's staff. Of course, they do it with the expectation that they will then be able to secure contracts to prepare reports on the policy issue at hand for the clients. And the swamp gains more and more power.

One needs only to look at the outsourced government contracts to begin to understand how the lobbyists, with help from the unelected paper pushers, make policy-making a dirty business. For swamp drain-ing to be more than a phase, it must begin with stripping the power of the lobbyists, the corrupt politicians, and the corrupt staffers who are motivated by greed. Congressional representatives should work in concert with one another to pool resources to help them make policy decisions and rely less on the reports and analyses from those with a profit-gaining motive. Citizens must insist that policy-making be pure and purely in their interests.

But accountability is not all. The sharp rise of the swamp's power creates the need for a serious discussion about whether "congressman for life" also contributes to ensuring that the spoils of corruption are a motivating factor for candidates to run. This discussion requires a serious reading of the facts and circumstances rather than a simplistic default position that a lack of term limits is unconstitutional.

Draining the Swamp Requires Term Limits

It is true that the Constitution doesn't provide for term limits for members of the House or Senate; originally, it didn't do so for the president, either. After two terms, George Washington had had enough and decided that he would leave office. It was his action that arguably set the precedent for future presidents to do the same. While there were no formal term limits, there was a gentlemen's agreement that held steady until 1940, when Franklin Delano Roosevelt upended the apple cart and ran for (and won) a third term. After Roosevelt won a fourth term in 1944 and died in office a few months later, Americans saw the need to formalize the gentlemen's agreement. The political tide had shifted in favor of term limits. Congress acted passed the Twenty-Second Amendment a couple of years later, in 1947, and the states ratified it in 1951.

I understand and support the need not to limit the power of elected officials. However, our country is in crisis. A major part of that crisis has been caused by the power grab by elected officials. Being a member of Congress is desirable to many not because it is noble, but because it is an opportunity to enrich themselves while in office and after they leave office. Members of Congress have no bosses to whom they report, except maybe around election time. They have no performance goals, no measures of success, and no obligation to vote in the interests of their constituents.

Some argue that the people retain the right to vote members of Congress out of office. In theory, yes. But in recent years, the American electorate has become so disengaged from politics that bothering to vote in congressional elections is not a priority. The fact is that despite calls for reform, the vast majority of members of Congress are easily re-elected. The president supports term limits for Congress, as indicated by his tweeting this on April 30, 2018:

Donald J. Trump
@realDonaldTrump

I recently had a terrific meeting with a bipartisan group of freshman lawmakers who feel very strongly in favor of Congressional term limits. I gave them my full support and endorsement for their efforts. #DrainTheSwamp[6]

The president has it right. We have come to the point where we can no longer sit by and simply expect elected officials to be honest. They have proven to us that there is no honor among thieves and that since too many in the republic prefer a hands-off approach, they will damn well do what they please. Moreover, they understand that they can act with impunity and that too many of us will accept that.

I am a diehard conservative, and I do not believe in a liberal interpretation of the Constitution. I also believe that the framers never intended that the republic should become a slave to corruption. Although drastic, term limits ought to be something that we have a vigorous debate about, given our current reality.

Term limits will cut off the head of the snake of the professional member of Congress who serves thirty, forty, or even fifty-plus years in Washington. It would blow up the cartel of long-serving members

---

6 "Sorry, Mr. President: Term limits for Congress are still not going to happen," Amber Phillips, Washington Post, May 1, 2018, https://www.washingtonpost.com/news/the-fix/wp/2018/05/01/sorry-trump-term-limits-for-congress-are-still-not-going-to-happen/?utm_term=.6ade5fe1d601

of Congress and lobbyists who now rule the capital. It would assist in the fight against ever-higher taxes and spending. It would help restore the sort of citizen legislature the founders intended.

We simply do not realize that the current power structure is a deadly combination of the mob, drug lords, and union bosses. This will not end well. My critics say that corruption used to be worse and that at least we no longer have smoke-filled back rooms in which decisions are made. This is a stupid comment. The issue is not where the corruption takes place; it is that it does take place. So smoke-filled back rooms have been replaced by K Street lobbying firms, garden parties in Georgetown, and yacht rides on the Potomac. The name has changed, but the game remains the same.

Conclusion

Draining the swamp means that we must all return to eradicating division and understanding the fundamentals of what has become a very fragile republic. It requires an understanding of civics and what this great nation should be. I don't subscribe to the intentionally misleading spin that "making America great again" somehow harks to racism and exclusion. Instead, I believe that MAGA refers to a need to take back control of the republic from the swamp dwellers who rape and pillage America for their own gains. It means active citizen participation. It requires that we understand what divides us so that we can fix it, and that we call on the media to report the news and not tell us what we should think.

The nation's capital has become so infested by the politics of corruption that Dick and Debbie Salt of the Earth do not see themselves in America. Instead, they see themselves living in an alternate reality that is not sustainable. The politics of destruction in America has reached a fever pitch, and only we the citizens of America can move from fever pitch to solutions. The swamp dwellers, corrupt politicians, media, and lobbyists will not address the issue because it is not in their self-interest to do so. Taking back our country from the jaws of the swamp creatures requires that we the people do so. It is time that we seriously consider term limits. It is the only way to sustain the political system of the republic.

The question is, do we have the internal and external fortitude to do so? And will we do so? Or will we continue to do what we have done to get us to this point...moan, complain, and do nothing to change? Our country, our choice.

CHAPTER 6

American Education:
No Reform, Just Entrenchment

Our American Education System Penalizes
Free Thought and Expression

We have an education system that neither teaches nor rewards free thought. Instead, it penalizes free thought and expression.

At the risk of stating the obvious, let me say that the American public education system needs radical reform. Despite efforts by liberal-leaning think tanks, teachers unions, and others, the American education system continues to graduate noncritical thinkers and sends sheep to the slaughter in an increasingly complex world.

When I was a university professor, I was stunned by the number of students who simply lacked the ability to think critically. These students had an uncanny ability to repeat what they heard, but they could not deconstruct a sentence, pose a credible argument, or take a well-fortified position on any issue. They were full of sound bites and phrases, and they spoke from a place of ignorance rather than of information.

Good teachers make a difference. The problem is that there simply are not enough of them, and far too many school boards have become bastions of political fermentation rather than being concerned about what children are learning. Many school boards and/or school system chiefs are in the business of awarding contracts for learning products and educational pedagogy to their friends and/or political contributors, who then give them kickbacks. But, corruption in the education system is but one of the issues that makes many Americans so angry. Liberals argue that the issue is pumping more and more money into the system. But, they provide no evidence that additional money is the answer and they ignore the corruption issues, the cheating scandals and the school board officials who take kickbacks for sitting on the boards of companies that do business with the school systems which they lead. The vexing issue and the source of anger in the public education system is besieged by excessive spending and yet it underperforms. To be sure, there is widespread public support for public education yet the system has been so heavily influenced by liberal groups that care less about education and more about power. Thus, anger is not unwarranted. In facts, it is necessary. But, it needs to be anger matched by action and accountability. In the context of education, the anger is not only at the public education level, it is increasingly occurring on college campuses where liberal professors are more in the business of indoctrination and less in the business of education. I know that issue first hand, I was a college professor on three liberal college campuses.

Liberal College Professors Who Indoctrinate Have Led to a Conservative Backlash

The rise of liberal elite professors on college and university campuses all across the country has resulted in a fierce conservative backlash.

First, Conservative students, in my experience as a professor, challenged liberal doctrine pushed by liberals. Second, were it not for liberal "education," conservatives would not have protested so much on campuses. Here is the reality. All college professors have political opinions. I am not suggesting that my colleagues check those opinions at the door. However, discernment is critical to being an effective professor. This means that a college professor should keep those opinions to themselves, and provide a teaching environment in which students can argue, think for themselves and form their own opinions. Liberal college professors have so long dominated American College campuses for so long that they have created a culture of liberalism that has caused a clash and anger that is long overdue. Far too many liberal college professors college is no longer the free market place of ideas where we introduce students to the major thinking and theories in their field of study. Thereafter, we encourage them to think for themselves and reach their own conclusions. Anger on college campuses is caused in part by the fact that liber dogma and shutting out conservatives or even moderate voices is now the norm.

The reality is that school systems are responsible for producing students who can memorize but not think. Sheep eventually end up eating democracy for lunch.

I am a graduate of Columbia University and taught at Cornell University and Georgetown University. All of these institutions are overwhelmingly staffed by liberal professors who see their purpose as indoctrination and adoption of liberal ideology.

For example, I distinctly recall that as I sat in my Introduction to Human Rights class in the graduate program at Columbia, there was a panel discussion in which liberal professors railed against the views of conservatives in the human rights field. I recall the panelists' imploring us to reject what they called a hate-filled conservative agenda regarding human rights. I raised my hand and pointed out that these bra-burning liberals had no right to tell me how to think about human rights. Their only response: bras are too expensive to burn.

At Georgetown, I did many Fox News interviews. The director of communications for the university at the time complained that my appearances were too harsh and that he was afraid I was speaking for Georgetown on these shows. Largely, my appearances involved a critique of the policies of the Obama administration, which the facts showed would not be helpful. Universities preach academic freedom all the time. However, that freedom is free only if you agree with their liberal points of view. I was on the faculty with the liberal college professor Michael Eric Dyson. a New York Times contributing opinion writer, and a contributing editor of The New Republic, and of ESPN's The Undefeated website. At the time, Dyson spent quite a bit of time on the liberal bastion MSNBC. He was not taken to task for his many appearances nor were many of my liberal colleagues who consistently and without apology contributed to liberal outlets.

For too many liberal professors, universities are a "safe space" where Karl Marx is a hero, Fidel Castro is an icon, all whites are racists, blacks should vote for Democrats as a matter of course, and the roads to Hell are paved with dead conservatives. Many liberal college professors have morphed into progressives and are rebranding themselves. The problem, however, is that the name has changed but the game remains the same. "Progressive" and "inclusive" on many college campuses are mutually exclusive. One can be progressive only if one rejects conservatism and embraces mind control.

In my view, colleges and universities were created for the simple purpose of creating and nurturing a broad and inclusive environment supported by a passion for learning, thinking, and growing. They were not designed to be taken over by liberal and progressive hacks whose agenda is to force-feed young minds the professors' pabulum. As professors, our job is to introduce to students the ideas that are germane to their fields of study without gloss. However, on many college campuses, truth, free thinking, and ideas have become a casualty of the knowledge war that we find ourselves in. Division among college professors means that the subjects we are supposed to teach are now secondary to ad hominem attacks on the message and the messengers.

From my experience as a student at a liberal university and as a professor, the attacks on both conservative students and professors are nonsensical and hypocritical. The result has been many students' rejecting this institutional mayhem and moving to the right politically. "Liberals gone wild" has become the best recruiting tool for the conservative movement on campus. I am not sure, though, how sustainable this is. College campuses need to get back to the mission of education and to being contributors to the free marketplace of ideas, and need to get out of the business of sowing division. The liberal takeover of education spells doom for the republic—mark my words.

Be Afraid Be Very Afraid: The Federal Government Enters Education

Whenever you hear that the federal government's role in something is increasing, you should be very afraid. In the case of education, the federal government's role is increasing.

> *"President Carter created the Department of Education in 1979 because he was forced to do so by the once-powerful National Education Association (NEA) and other teachers' unions. It was clear that federalizing education would do nothing to improve it. President Reagan came into office in 1980 promising to abolish it. He called it Jimmy Carter's 'little boondoggle.'"*[1]

---

[1] Chris Edwards, Tax Policy Studies, The Cato Institute, quoted in "The Plan, Day Three: Abolish the Department of Education," transcript from *Glenn Beck*, April 14, 2010

However, at the time, the unions had a stranglehold on Washington, and so the lack of political will to abolish simply was not there. "[The] funding started in 1965 when it was part of another department. And all the states unionized their workforces in the 1960s. The teachers' unions got a lot of power starting in the 1960s,"[2] and they have used that power for evil, not good. That is, rather than focusing on helping local school systems thrive, the unions focused on nationalizing education—an approach that in large part is responsible for the failure of the American education system. Their alignment with the far left doomed any chance of making real change. Most of their contributions and "get out the vote" efforts have been focused on the left.

Despite the notion that the department would improve test scores, it did not. Instead, it created massive regulations and mandates that had nothing to do with education. Its budgets were bloated, and it did not improve test scores. Education is a divisive issue in America in part because special interest groups have hijacked it for their own political agendas. It is clear that the current American education system is a laughingstock. Despite the billions of dollars that taxpayers have spent on K-12 education over the past several decades, test scores have not improved, and children can't think critically.

> *"Examining the full picture, data from the U.S. Bureau of Economic Analysis and the U.S. Department of Education shows that inflation-adjusted government spending on higher education increased by 23 percent from 2008 to 2016, hitting a record high of $183 billion in 2016. On a per-student basis in the same period, this spending increased by 16 percent and also reached an all-time high of more than $9,000 per student."[3]*

---

[2] Ibid.

[3] "Government Spending on Education Is Higher than Ever. And for What?" Stuart Shepard and James Agresti, The Foundation for Economic Education, March 1, 2018, fee.org, https://fee.org/articles/government-spending-on-education-is-higher-than-ever-and-for-what/

But why has government spending on education increased so much? First, there is mass corruption in the market for textbooks that schools buy every year. Often, these contracts are awarded to the friends and associates of school board members or school superintendents. For example, in Baltimore County, Maryland, former superintendent Shaun Dallas Dance was charged with perjury for concealing his personal profit from an educational company that was awarded a contract by his school system.[4] Dance is not alone. A former Los Angeles school board superintendent with an annual salary of six hundred thousand dollars was charged with corruption and conflicts of interest.[5]

I could spend an entire chapter detailing the scandals, but that is not the point of this chapter. It is simply to illustrate how the billions of taxpayer dollars infused by the federal government into local schools have fed and continue to feed corruption.

A major reason that the American public education system is a black hole is that the federal government came riding in on a Trojan horse promising better outcomes. Instead, it has delivered wasteful spending increases and a morass of regulations, and is a willing accomplice before, during, and after the fact in destroying what was once the purview of the states.

Let's also not forget that there are alternatives such as school choice. However, the teachers' unions and their allies have colluded openly to use children as pawns and continue division to gain fat pensions for their members and amass campaign contributions for liberals so that the unions have power. Children be damned.

---

[4] "Former Baltimore County Schools Leader Charged with Perjury," Natasha Singer and Danielle Ivory, *New York Times*, Jan. 23, 2018, https://www.nytimes.com/2018/01/23/technology/baltimore-schools-perjury.html

[5] "Superintendent with Outrageous Salary Charged with Corruption," CBS Los Angeles, Aug. 31, 2017, https://losangeles.cbslocal.com/2017/08/31/superintendent-excessive-salary-charged-corruption/

Why has education become such a divisive issue? Should we not be concerned about the education of all of our children, rather than creating a system that has been consumed by the federal government in which choice is not an option? The American education system is controlled in large part by the federal government and its policy wonks. This does not happen just at the state and local levels.

Colleges and Universities

In fact, colleges and universities are also under the federal government's thumb.

The sprawling and highly invasive Department of Education has amassed almost absolute power and control over higher education, even though the voters have never elected anyone from that department to any position of power. It is yet another example of how Washington, D.C., has taken the place of parents and teachers in deciding how people should be educated. The Department of Education has become the nanny state, and its power-grabbing, agenda-setting minions are only too glad to use that unearned power.

The power-and-control model is toxic to learning. Rather than being an agency of change and education, the department has hijacked the system in an attempt to destroy the ability of colleges and universities to fulfill the mission of educating students, shoring up their skills, and teaching them to think critically and become contributing members of society. One can simply look at the steady and never-ending mandates published by the department.

But it does not stop with the publication of mandates. The mandates are often so nonsensical and poorly written that the department must then issue social guidance that purports to amend or clarify the gibberish it wrote in the first place. As a general rule, the mandates tend to be about two thousand pages of text. So in addition to reading and analyzing the two thousand pages, a college or university must read the excessive pages of the guidance. Even after the mandates and clarifications, colleges and universities still find themselves confused, and the investigators may fine them for failing to comply with often incomprehensible regulations and "clarifying" guidance.

Any college or university, private or public, that receives federal government funds must comply with the endless federal regulations. Federal government funds include research dollars and federal financial aid. Cynics say that institutions which don't wish to be subject to the regulations should simply not take any federal funds. This is an impractical and illogical "argument," for the following reasons.

First, many students are on federal financial aid, and a college or university that is ineligible for federal financial aid will not attract those students, so it might as well shut its doors.

Second, federal research dollars are a significant source of income for colleges and universities. They cannot simply refuse them.

Finally, such "arguments" are a distraction from the real issue, which is that federal government regulations determine who is admitted, what is taught, and how it is taught. Colleges and universities spend untold funds hiring staff to keep up with the regulations, thus diverting funds from education.

This chapter explores and analyzes the fundamental problem of federalizing education, and exposes the fundamental flaws in a declining education system and a workforce that has led to a significant skill gap. The chapter also explores strategies for returning control to the states and proposes alternatives for reforming the system.

An Educator's Perspective

I am an educator by training. I have taught at the undergraduate and graduate levels at Cornell University, Georgetown University, and

City University of New York, among other institutions. I am also an employer who experiences firsthand the lack of skills many students bring to the workplace. I have also served as a consultant to the National Education Association. So I know of what I speak.

The reality is that the American education system, in its current form, is continuing to fail students, largely for the following reasons:

- Teachers are not themselves properly educated.
- There is an emphasis on "teaching to the test."
- The education system as a whole is rife with political interference.
- Students are not being taught how to analyze key concepts.
- Special-interest groups have more power and influence in education than parents do.

There is a need for drastic and sustained action to get the federal government out of education to the extent that it is currently involved and return control to the states. National standards are limited in what they can do. All they can do is provide guidance. However, too many special interest groups are looking at them as a cure for what ails the American education system. Simply put, these standards have taken over educational policy thinking and are the foundation of curriculum and pedagogy. However, parents are left out of the equation, and the education of their children is being dictated by educational paper pushers. This is the worst possible outcome.

It wasn't always this way. In fact, prior to the 1980s and early 1990s, testing and education standards were purely the business of the states, and it worked just fine. But many in Washington thought the states were simply too stupid to handle this task—a task that they had been handling quite well before the intrusion of the federal government. The agenda was clear: the unions and their allies wanted to indoctrinate, and not educate, students. The paper pushers in Washington felt that on the issue of education, they knew best, not the parents or the "local yokels." So they began a thinly veiled attack on local control and disguised it as education reform. My question remains, who were they to reform the way locals went about education? This so-called need for national standards should have been our first clue. Why do we need national standards?

American national standards have never changed anything for the better. In fact, America is made up of several independent states, and the issues and challenges in each state are local ones. A national standards debate is code for the federal government's controlling those things that states should be controlling. Moreover, it is an attempt to distract from the real problems in the American education system. Whenever the term "national standards" is used, I hear the phrase, "I am from the government, and I am here to help." Which means it will not end well.

The education system is drowning because of poor teacher training, disengaged parents, poorly disciplined students, parents who themselves are products of a failed education system and so are unable to help their children, testing replacing critical thinking, poor teacher pay, top-heavy administration, and the list goes on and on. These are the issues—some stupid and meaningless discussion about national standards is not the issue. How will national standards solve these problems? They can't.

These problems are at the heart and soul of America's failing public education system. National standards such as testing worsen the problem. National standards seek to replace parents with paper pushers and have those paper pushers decide what students learn, how they learn it, what they will be tested on, and by whom. The federal government was never meant to be a pseudo parent. School boards are locally elected. However, national standards intend to usurp that by taking control of what local school boards do, and they result in what was never envisioned in our system of government: making the Department of Education a national school board. I simply do not buy the empty argument that this is not about nationalizing education; instead, it is about setting aspirational targets for excellence, not about standardizing. Since when has the federal government set a standard of excellence for anything? National standards are a hostile takeover of education, with local school boards being a casualty. The paper pushers in Washington will use these standards as a way of controlling the agenda and deciding that only those local governments which comply with the government's idiotic funding formulas will be given the funding to fulfill the national agenda set not by parents but by nonelected paper pushers.

I have yet to see any national standard that addresses the issues I have outlined. Rather, the standards read more like talking points from unions and special interest groups seeking to advance their agendas.

State control of education has worked well primarily because the locals are on the ground and can and do engage parents to help meet the educational needs of their children. Local education is not exclusively testing-focused. Teachers do more than simply prepare students to pass the national standards in reading and math. Local control puts its emphasis on the whole student rather than the race to the test scores. By becoming slaves to national standards, we are not improving learning, we are stifling it. The Department of Education, as currently configured, destroys the connection between local control and learning in favor of a feigned "race to the top." This is a losing race, in which the streets on which the race is being run are littered with the deaths of learning, teacher evaluations, school improvement strategies, and accountability. This so-called reform is actually retrenchment, in which the Department of Education is king and the locals are the subjects. I thought we had gotten away from royal rule.

Let's be clear: properly read and understood, the attempt to nationalize educational standards would undermine the success that local school boards and parents have had in education, with no clear choice or alternative.

Solutions

So what can federal policy do to help the locals?

First, stay out of any attempt to micromanage local education. Taxpayers have spent billions of dollars on developing research and tools that may be helpful to local school boards and governments. Why not engage the locals in a discussion about what tools they need? Those tools should be offered, not mandated.

Second, demystify the funding process so the locals are able to understand them. The goal of funding should be to ensure that local school boards have maximum flexibility in applying those funds. Keep in mind that the states provide taxpayer dollars to the federal government, and the federal government gives it back to the states through complex and oftentimes nonsensical funding mechanisms.

Finally, consider the root cause of the failure of K-12 education: it teaches students what to think, not how to think, and colleges and universities are no better.

State policy should advance systemic reforms that better align power and incentives with educational outcomes, including enhanced accountability and parental empowerment through educational choice. This is simple common sense and void of any special interest, and is driven by outcomes. The current educational chaos is driven by an unreasonable effort to standardize, not reform. No one is fooled by the rebranding of the word "reform" when the real issue is power and control through efforts led by an entrenched special interest lobby.

The solutions I have presented so far get to the core issues underlying the hijacking of the American education system. Education is an issue that affects all Americans, and so the strategy has to change and sustain the system at its core. Buzzwords, talking points, and meaningless "reform" efforts have to be replaced with action. Let's implement this combination of reforms, so that Americans can better address the core issues that continue to drive division, ignore local efforts, reward mediocrity, and create a federal system that is designed to survive just for the sake of surviving.

Education Reform: A Brief Overview

Education reform is nothing new. The issue has never really been about reform in its truest sense. Instead, it has been about standards and testing. In America, we love to avoid difficult topics by giving them names to make people believe that we have addressed them—for example, "education reform." Education reform is simply a politically correct term that seeks to disguise naked political ideology.

To add more context, I am including a brief overview of the history of those efforts.

Today's education reform discussion has been shaped largely by two widely divergent visions of education. Those views still underpin the education reform discussion in America today. At the core of these views are the issues of standards and test scores. How the country responds to test scores and standards will be the genesis of the reform movement.

Education reform is both an educational issue and a political issue. Conservatives and many libertarians fundamentally believe in the free market and that education helps to secure the future of the free market. Thus, they found logic in the work of Chester "Checker" Finn Jr., assistant secretary of education in the Reagan administration.

For Finn, it wasn't about testing and standardization of test scores. The approach of embracing test scores was, in his view, a false choice. It also did not address the real issues. Instead it was a thinly disguised political ploy to address testing and not choice. Free marketers understand the danger of removing choice. For definitional and illustrative purposes, I point to this explanation of choice; I then put this into the context of education:

> *"Freedom of choice in the marketplace means there is a voluntary exchange between buyer and seller. Coercion and force are absent from this process. The freedom of choice is not influenced by law or by criminal activity. When the freedom of choice is exercised by all market participants, their collective actions will determine what is produced, what is consumed, and the price at which the exchange will take place. This is the natural outcome when freedom of choice is present in the marketplace.*
>
> *When those who govern attempt to legislate our freedom of choice, the voluntary exchange process becomes corrupted. If this occurs the markets will no longer function as a free and natural process. Prices will become distorted and your right to freedom of choice in the marketplace will be sacrificed.*
>
> *The use of the word dictator to describe someone who would limit the choices of others is worthy of note. When those who govern limit our freedom of choice in the marketplace, they have become dictators over the people."*[6]

In the context of education, parents buy the commodity of education by paying tax dollars; thus, they should have freedom of choice when it comes to what offerings they purchase for their families without restrictions and the usurpation of choice by the government. It is just that simple.

---

[6] "The Freedom of Choice—a Free Market Concept," Freedom Economics, http://www.learnfreedomeconomics.com/the-freedom-of-choice/

For Finn, the only real reform and the natural outcome in education had to be a shift to school choice, which he advocated because it got to the heart of the issue: educational choice. Without choice as the foundation, Finn correctly argued, education cannot ever be truly changed in a free market economy. Of course, it requires that parents be informed choosers; that, as in any market, consumers must be able to make informed choices in order for the market to be effective in promoting quality products and services. From the standpoint of education, the local-market consumers know the market best, and so it is asinine to assert that choice should be made at the federal level. While Finn did not dismiss the idea of testing altogether, he saw it as a tool and not an outcome.

Within the education context, Finn argued, parental consumers would need to be informed by standards-based tests developed by the states in order to ensure their rigor and reliability. To Finn's mind, these standards-based tests were but a measure that would be localized and allow the consumers (that is, the parents) to use a tool that could assess quality. They were not a solution but a tool for the informed consumer. That tool would serve as, for example, a compare-the-choices model that consumers so readily use in making purchases. Parents armed with this information may decide that something does not work for their children and then make other market-based decisions, such as moving to a different school district, proposing curricular choices, and so on.

Not satisfied with Finn's rationale and subsequent argument, Marshall "Mike" Smith, former undersecretary of education in the Clinton administration, developed his own philosophy. Curriculum standards were the answer. Such standards would be developed by those who knew best (that is, policy elites), not parents. The federal government would interpret decisions made by states in the areas of testing; textbook adoption; teacher preparation; teacher certification, evaluation, and training; goals and timetables for school test score improvement; and state accountability based on those goals and timetables.

But wait a minute: why would the states need the federal government to do this? Why could they not do it on their own? The fatal flaw in this approach is not that difficult to spot, given the federalization of education this philosophy espouses: the standards adopted would be federal and not state standards. But don't worry, the policy makers are from the federal government, and they are here to help.

For those who believe the federal government is the answer to all that ails us, standards and testing were not a tool but a solution. Smith and others of his ilk branded their use "systemic reform." In other words, this replaced local control over education with federal control over education. According to Smith, curriculum standards in and of themselves are not tools, they are solutions. All of the work on education reform has resulted in no reform at all. It has resulted in division, children who have learned very little in terms of how to analyze and think, no accountability, loss of state control, and the erosion of education standards.

Like it or not, we live in a global society where we are competing with countries that are outperforming us. So the inability to compete is not an option. We have not answered some very basic questions, choosing instead to migrate to an outdated and ineffective model of political pandering and clinging to outdated tools in and of themselves as solutions. The common man has very little say about how his children are educated, as the policy elites, in their view, own the issues, the debate, and the outcome. This cannot and will not work. It is outdated and based not on reform but on protecting the status quo. The American education system needs disruption, not merely tweaking at the edges. This begins with asking the questions the policy wonks and paper pushers have not asked, because they are afraid of the answers. These questions include:

- What is the purpose of the public education system in America?
- Who owns the system?
- How does the free market inform decision making in our system, if at all?
- Why are parents shut out of crucial decision-making roles?
- Why can't our children better analyze problems?
- Why are we so comfortable with teaching to the test?
- Are our teachers trained to meet today's educational challenges?
- How do we resolve the state-federal dilemma?

These are not the only questions, but they are baseline questions for which we need to have answers so that we can take action. In addition, the education debate is consumed by assumptions that simply prohibit progress. Among the areas that are rife with assumptions is how education is managed, funded, designed, and overseen. Those debating policy and making decisions believe that they must come up with something new. In theory, this is fine, but how can we do this if we don't learn from past change efforts? Not only do we need to know what has worked, but we need to know why it worked. We also need to know what has failed and why it has failed. We don't have measurable outcomes in large part because we are afraid that those outcomes will be dismal. This is true. But the issue is not that they are dismal; it is *why* they are dismal. Teachers' unions do not come honestly to this debate. They simply cannot accept the reality that this is a mess they have created and nurtured for their own gain. As an educator who believes in outcomes, I find that in the context of the American education system, there are some basic benchmarks that educational charlatans and their sycophants refuse to embrace in earnest.

Academic performance as measured by achievement tests, completion rates, and international comparisons, rather than by spending, intentions, or equity of access must be the principal benchmark for assessing the success or failure of American schools. This is not meant to dismiss the equity issue. It is to suggest that equity lies at the core of all of the benchmarks rather than in opposition to the benchmarks.

I have discussed the problem. So what are the solutions?

Many say teachers are underpaid, and believe that is at the core of the problem. I am not sure that issue is at the core. I agree that teacher pay is an issue; however, I am not an advocate of simply granting increases to all teachers. The granting of increases should be done as it is in the marketplace. It should be based on merit.

I believe the oppressive union contracts that have long dominated teacher pay and that despise merit pay should be voided. The reason they oppose merit pay has nothing to do with children or education. It is rooted in the unions' egotistical and self-serving desire to control and dominate education without regard for what is best for education. They wish to take union dues to elect their Democratic masters. This must end.

What must also end is the unions' desire to reward teaching in place rather than quality of teaching. By this, I mean unions could not care less about the quality of teaching. Instead, they believe that the longer a teacher has been teaching, the more that teacher should be paid. Tenure over quality is the bane of the American public schools' existence.

In addition, unions fight holding teachers accountable at every turn. This is evidence of the fact that they are willing accomplices before, during, and after the fact in the destruction of the American public education system. When it comes to keeping the American public education system mediocre, unions bear a significant part of the responsibility. They simply do not believe that teachers should be evaluated and compensated based on performance. Teaching under union control is one of the few professions in America in which there are no consequences for poor performance. Where quality is of no moment and the longer one has been employed, the harder it is to fire that person. And we wonder why American public education is in such shambles.

It is now time to set standards. However, the federal government should have no role whatsoever in setting such standards. Instead, these standards must be locally and state-based. The Tenth Amendment to the U.S. Constitution states: "The powers not delegated to the United States by the Constitution, nor prohibited by it to the States, are reserved to the States respectively, or to the people."

It is therefore crystal clear that the power to create schools and a system for education belongs exclusively to individual states, rather than to the central national government. Today, all fifty states provide public schooling, as they should, but we should have fifty approaches to education based locally on the needs of the individual states.

The concepts of federalism should apply to education, just as they should to most government-related agencies.

Local school districts should have the greatest power to determine effective and acceptable standards without interference from the heavy hand of either a large bureaucratic federal government or unions. Until this happens, the American public education system will continue to go to Hell in a handbasket. Our children will continue to be undereducated, we will lose our competitive edge, and mediocrity will define us. There is no excuse for going down this path.

Unions Oppose Choice

Since the 1980s, the informed-school-choice movement has gained momentum. The field of K-12 education has witnessed a welcome surge in interest concerning school choice and charter schools. As is its right, each state has taken its own approach to choice. The movement got a big boost when, during the presidential campaign of 2016, then-candidate

Trump assured that his administration would provide federal money to help students attend a school of their choice. Secretary of education Betsy DeVos has worked in the choice-and-charter-school movement since her introduction to the field of education.

While the movement has gained momentum, the unions have, of course, reared their ugly heads in violent opposition. They did not ask parents what they thought, because in the minds of union members, the unions know best:

> *"The American Federation for Children's third annual National School Choice Poll, released Thursday [in January 2017], found that more than two-thirds of likely 2018 voters support the idea of school choice. Nearly three-quarters of respondents, 72 percent, favor a federal tax credit scholarship, a proposal most recently intro-duced in Congress in 2015, and 51 percent support President-elect Donald Trump's proposal to shift $20 billion in federal education funding to promote school choice."*[7]

Polls have consistently shown that parents and communities over-whelmingly support school choice. Understanding the needs and desires of parents to determine what is best for their children is simply not complicated. Unions are not ultimately responsible for the success of students; parents are. Yet unions have taken on the role of determin-ing the role of shaping education regardless of what parents think.

The problem with this, of course, is that unions have a different motive than parents do. Their motive is protecting the jobs, pensions, and salaries of their members, regardless of whether children are edu-cated or not. They are beholden to the left and know that the more money they give to the left, the more power they will have. Teacher

---

[7] "Poll—75% of Millennials Support School Choice; Majority of Americans Like Trump's $20 billion Plan," Kate Stringer, The 74, www.the74Million.org, Jan. 12, 2017, https://www.the74million.org/article/poll-75-percent-of-millennials-support-school-choice-majority-of-americans-like-trumps-20-billion-plan/

competency, proficiency, and readiness to educate students is of no concern to unions; job security is. If it were true, as the unions say it is, that their motivation is the education of children, then why do they oppose charter schools? Why do they oppose an open, competitive marketplace?

The answer is simple. If they have competition in which competency, pay based on performance, measurable outcomes, and the like were present, parents would flee in droves. As a result, the unions would lose market share, lose dues money, lose influence, and cease to exist.

Let's not be single-minded and myopic in our approach to fixing the mess the unions have given us. We must eradicate the power and control of the unions that have infected our public education system.

The presence and influence of unions in education is but one of the issues that has fired up Americans. The other is the increasing involvement of the courts in rendering decisions that impact education. Education has always been considered a local issue. It is worth noting that The Supreme Court of the United States largely ignored making rulings in school cases until after World War Two. Since then however, the Court has made many rulings on education cases. I offer the following two cases as examples of the power the court wields over education and why both liberals and conservatives view the court as an essential battleground and target of anger. The following two cases are illustrative of two seminal cases that affect education. They are seminal because they show the broad power the court has taken in rendering school decisions.

San Antonio Independent School District v. Rodriguez (1972)

The San Antonio Independent School District in Texas was funded in part by local property taxes. The District sued the state on behalf of the students in its district, arguing that since property taxes were relatively low in the area, students at the public schools were at a huge disadvantage and received substandard education given that the rich parents had higher property taxes and thus more money for education. The Plaintiff's theory of the case rests on the Equal Protection Clause of the 14th Amendment which they said, mandates equal funding among school districts, but the court ultimately rejected their claim. It held that there is no fundamental right to education guaranteed in the Constitution, and that the Equal Protection Clause doesn't require exact "equality or precisely equal advantages" among school districts.

This case illustrates that the court will intervene in decisions affecting education. It is also one of the reasons why the importance of who sits on The Supreme Court is so consequential to many Americans.

Tinker v. Des Moines (1969)

The Vietnam War tore the fabric of America apart. During its most virulent times, students in the Des Moines Independent Community School District in Iowa wore black armbands to school as an expression of their dissatisfaction with U.S. foreign policy. The district responded and put in place a rule prohibiting the armbands as part of a larger dress code, and students challenged the ban as a violation of the Free Speech Clause of the First Amendment. The Court agreed with the students and struck down the ban, saying that the school has to prove that the conduct or speech "materially and substantially interferes" with school operations in order to justify the ban. This case is notable for its impact on First Amendment jurisprudence regarding distinctions between conduct and speech, as well as for its extension of free speech protections to students.

In the context of educational policy, Supreme Court decisions are inevitable. Thus, we have to get into the trenches and work in tandem with parents to change thinking and behavior. "Local control is the answer" is just a slogan. Parents must look at whom they elect to the local school boards in an attempt to determine whether these elected officials are well steeped in the local educational needs.

Parents themselves may also wish to consider running for and being elected to the local school boards. The reality is that the point of entry for many budding politicians is the school board. The question for parents is whether their election to school boards is what would be right for the education of students at large.

Conclusion

At the risk of stating the obvious, the American public education system is in a death spiral. It is time to address this head-on. Both conservatives and liberals have an obligation to look at the effects of the massive federal intrusion into education as well as the role of unions in causing the decline. The issue has led to a divided America because the discussion and efforts are so mired in politics and ideology that no action is being taken. Posturing and shouting have become the tools of choice. We are losing our competitive edge while those who can make a difference sit back as spectators of a bad game.

I, for one, am not impressed by the reform efforts because they have resulted in papers and studies and at best have tinkered around the edges and retained the status quo. Sustained change requires decisive action and disruption, qualities that the special interest groups lack. Meanwhile, parents are not as involved in change as they should be. On education, it makes no sense to ask for whom the bell tolls. It tolls for thee.

CHAPTER 7

White Supremacy and Black Lives: Never the Two Shall Meet

For the past five years, no two movements have captured the attention of the American public more than Black Lives Matter and the alt-right. Seemingly operating on opposite ends of a spectrum that seeks to codify the values this country is based on (most specifically, liberty and justice for all), Black Lives Matter and the alt-right have polarized the public discourse on race relations in America.

Of course, there are always groups that polarize the public discourse in America. We are a country that values the First Amendment and the right to speak freely. So what's the big deal with these groups? The big deal with these groups is that they are further evidence that America's soul is deeply troubled.

* * * * *

What exactly is Black Lives Matter? Here's one definition:

"The psychosis of whiteness is that it centers itself always. And when it is de-centered, when a group of people—but specifically black people, I think there's something about black people being visible or black people getting some threat of power that shakes up white people and their whiteness, that shakes up their experience of what should be true. I think there is a deep desire from even well-meaning white people to believe that they're not racist. But the reality is if you live in this country, if you're born and raised as a white person, then you most definitely are racist, and you have to contend with that. And I think Black Lives Matter puts it in peoples' face[s] to deal with not only the ways in which they benefit from whiteness and white supremacy, but deal with the ways in which black people actually must be free. And I think that's actually hard to contend with."[1]

And what is the alt-right? The Southern Poverty Law Center describes it this way:

"The Alternative Right is characterized by heavy use of social media and online memes. Alt-righters eschew "establishment" conservatism, skew young, and embrace white ethnonationalism as a fundamental value. In their own words:

'Martin Luther King Jr., a fraud and degenerate in his life, has become the symbol and cynosure of White Dispossession and the deconstruction of Occidental civilization. We must overcome!'

—Richard Spencer, National Policy Institute column,
January 2014

---

[1] Patrisse Khan-Cullors, with Asha Bandele, *When They Call You A Terrorist: A Black Lives Matter Memoir* (St. Martin's Press, 2018)

'Immigration is a kind of proxy war—and maybe a last stand—for White Americans, who are undergoing a painful recognition that, unless dramatic action is taken, their grandchildren will live in a country that is alien and hostile.'

—Richard Spencer, National Policy Institute column, February 2014

'Since we are fighting for nothing less than the biological survival of our race, and since the vast bulk of Jews oppose us, we need to err on the side of caution and have no association with Jews whatsoever. Any genuine Jewish well-wishers will understand, since they know what their people are like better than we ever can. Saving our race is something that we will have to do ourselves alone.'

—Greg Johnson, "White Nationalism and Jewish Nationalism," August 2011[2]

The influence of these groups can be seen in the hundreds and thousands of people who attend marches and rallies for each group's cause, and these groups can also be said to have influenced the perceptions and attitudes of the public in general. The presence, tactics, and actions of these groups have further stirred the simmering pot of a deeply divided nation. America used to be a place where keeping its soul pure was important. The presence of these groups shows us that America is involved in worshipping the idols of hate and bigotry, thus losing its humanistic soul.

Public perceptions about both movements indicate that there are mixed views about the movements, the messages each espouses, and general thoughts about race and race relations. For example:

---

[2] "Alt-Right," Southern Poverty Law Center, https://www.splcenter.org/fighting-hate/extremist-files/ideology/alt-right

- In a study conducted by Patrick S. Forscher and Nour Kteily among self-described alt-right adherents, on a scale of zero to one hundred—on which zero is not human and one hundred is fully human—white people scored 91.8 percent and black people scored 64.7 percent.[3]

- In the 2016 *USA Today*/Rock the Vote Millennial Poll, 34 percent expressed a favorable opinion of the alt-right, while 58 percent expressed a favorable opinion of Black Lives Matter.[4] In a 2017 poll conducted two weeks after the white supremacist march in Charlottesville, Virginia, 39 percent of respondents agreed that white people are currently "under attack" in the U.S., and 31 percent agreed that the white European heritage must be protected and preserved. Less than one-third of respondents indicated support for Black Lives Matter (37 percent opposed), and 6 percent expressed support for the alt-right.[5]

On questions regarding the alt-right and white nationalism, about one-fifth of respondents indicated neither support nor opposition to those groups.[6] The existence of the two movements together has brought a new level of discourse on race that has left the country reeling. How did we get here? How will it end?

---

[3] "A Psychological Profile of the Alt-Right," Patrick S. Forscher and Nour S. Kteily, Jan. 23, 2018, https://cdn.website-editor.net/84ddc9a4dfb04dd395a596949f857458/files/uploaded/Alt%20right%20preprint.pdf

[4] "Poll: How Millennials view BLM and the alt-right," Susan Page and Karina Shedrofsky, *USA Today*, Oct. 31, 2016

[5] "New Poll Finds Majority Oppose White Supremacists—Even While Sharing White Supremacist Views," Anne Branigin, The Root, Sept. 14, 2017. Poll conducted by *Reuters/Ipsos* in collaboration with the University of Virginia Center for Politics, https://www.theroot.com/new-poll-finds-majority-oppose-white-supremacists-even-1809072111

[6] "New Poll: Some Americans Express Troubling Racial Attitudes Even as Majority Oppose White Supremacists," University of Virginia Center for Politics, Sept. 14, 2017, http://www.centerforpolitics.org/crystalball/articles/new-poll-some-americans-express-troubling-racial-attitudes-even-as-majority-oppose-white-supremacists/

A Movement vs. an Ideology

Black Lives Matter began as a plea to recognize a truth—that there is a vast inequality experienced by African-Americans in the justice system compared to others, and this inequality was literally killing the community. The hashtag "#BlackLivesMatter" came into our national consciousness in 2013 after George Zimmerman was acquitted of the slaying of Trayvon Martin. The six-woman jury found George Zimmerman not guilty. They had three choices: to find Zimmerman guilty of second-degree murder; to find him guilty of the lesser charge of manslaughter; or to find him not guilty. The jurors deliberated for more than 16 hours total. The hashtag "#BlackLivesMatter" was a response to a decision that seemed to say that a white man's life was more important than a black man's life. It was also a reaction to a long-standing belief by many blacks and white liberals who believe that the police simply killed black men with wanton abandon. In addition to Martin, there is the case of Michael Brown.

Following the death of Michael Brown in Ferguson, Missouri, in 2014, individuals marched against the perceived brutality of law enforcement toward black men. "Black Lives Matter" became the rallying cry for African-Americans frustrated with the increased violence they were being confronted with in the criminal justice system, and a way to articulate that the deaths that have been occurring "are not a disconnected series of events but part of a national, systemic problem that flows out of institutional racism."[7]

Black Lives Matter identifies as a movement dedicated to affirming the lives of everyone: LGBTQI+, disabled, undocumented, ex-convicts, and women, especially those who have been marginalized within black liberation movements.

---

[7] "A Year Inside the Black Lives Matter Movement: How America's new generation of civil rights activists is mobilizing in the age of Trump," Touré, *Rolling Stone*, Dec. 7, 2017, https://www.rollingstone.com/politics/politics-news/a-year-inside-the-black-lives-matter-movement-204982/

"We are working for a world where Black lives are no longer systematically targeted for demise. We affirm our humanity, our contributions to this society, and our resilience in the face of deadly oppression. The call for Black lives to matter is a rallying cry for all Black lives striving for liberation."[8]

Members of the movement have organized chapters across the world with the mission "to build local power and to intervene in violence inflicted on Black communities by the state and vigilantes."[9]

Black Lives Matter affirms that all black lives matter. Adherents consider themselves:

"an ideological and political intervention in a world where Black lives are systematically and intentionally targeted for demise. It is an affirmation of Black folks' contributions to this society, our humanity, and our resilience in the face of deadly oppression."[10]

They operate under thirteen guiding principles: diversity, globalism, black women, black villages, loving engagement, restorative justice, collective value, empathy, queer affirming, unapologetically black, transgender affirming, black families, and intergenerational.[11] Members regularly organize and participate in rallies in locations where an injustice to members of the black community has occurred, including racial profiling and police brutality. In the first half of July 2017, more than 112 rallies had been held in eighty-eight cities.[12] Social media and "hashtag activism" allow members to connect to thousands of supporters.

---

[8] "About Herstory," BlackLivesMatter.com, retrieved May 7, 2018, https://blacklivesmatter.com/about/herstory/

[9] Ibid.

[10] Ibid.

[11] "Guiding Principles," Black Lives Matter, archived from the original Oct. 4, 2015, retrieved Feb. 26, 2017, https://blacklivesmatter.com/about/what-we-believe/

[12] "At Least 88 Cities Have Had Protests in the Past 13 Days Over Police Killings of Blacks," Jasmine C. Lee, Mykhyalyshyn, Iaryna, Omri, Rudy and Singhvi, Anjali, *New York Times*, July 16, 2016

BLM looks to achieve full inclusion and equal participation in society for all African-Americans. It seeks to do this by raising public/institutional awareness of racial disparities in law enforcement through marches, rallies, and public discourse. It is a nonviolent group that believes a more proactive, confrontational style is needed to get those in authority to listen to its issues. Adherents are looking for policy changes in law enforcement.

* * * * *

Alt-right is an ideology. According to the Anti-Defamation League, "the alt-right" is a "vague term actually encompass[ing] a range of people on the extreme right who reject mainstream conservatism in favor of forms of conservatism that embrace implicit or explicit racism or white supremacy."[13] According to the Southern Poverty Law Center, "the 'alt-right' is a set of far-right ideologies, groups, and individuals whose core belief is that 'white identity' is under attack by multicultural forces using 'political correctness' and 'social justice' to undermine white people and 'their' civilization."[14] The Associated Press describes the alt-right as an ideology

> *"...currently embraced by some white supremacists and white nationalists to refer to themselves and their ideology, which empha-sizes preserving and protecting the white race in the United States in addition to, or over, other traditional conservative positions such as limited government, low taxes and strict law-and-order."*[15]

---

[13] "Alt Right: A Primer about the New White Supremacy," Anti-Defamation League, retrieved: Jan. 26, 2018, https://www.adl.org/resources/backgrounders/alt-right-a-primer-about-the-new-white-supremacy

[14] "Alt-Right," Southern Poverty Law Center, retrieved May 7, 2018, https://www.splcenter.org/fighting-hate/extremist-files/ideology/alt-right

[15] "Writing about the 'alt-right,'" John Daniszewski, Associated Press, Nov. 26, 2016

In addition,

> *"the movement criticizes 'multiculturalism' and more rights for nonwhites, women, Jews, Muslims, gays, immigrants and other minorities. Its members reject the American democratic ideal that all should have equality under the law regardless of creed, gender, ethnic origin or race."*[16]

Richard Spencer is said to have coined the term: he describes it as a movement centered on white nationalism and as identity politics for white Americans and for Europeans around the world. Who is Richard Spencer? He was educated at both the University of Virginia and the University of Chicago. He formerly worked as a journalist at *The American Conservative.* He created alternativeright.com and is president of the National Policy Institute. According to Spencer, that organization advocates for "peaceful ethnic cleansing."[17]

The alt-right is seeking the creation of a "white Christendom, a group with indistinct geographical borders, but roughly including European peoples, from Iberia to the Caucasus, who were Christian as of a few hundred years ago."[18] Adherents are looking to bring this about through rallies and marches to highlight the perceived dismantling of white culture in America (and around the world). Violence and shootings are necessary to bring the natural order (white supremacy) back.

Perceptions/Misperceptions

Black Lives Matter as a movement has had its fair share of "what we believe versus what everyone else believes we believe." The fact is that

---

[16] Ibid.

[17] "About Richard Bertram Spencer In His Own Words," Southern Poverty Law Center, https://www.splcenter.org/fighting-hate/extremist-files/individual/richard-bertrand-spencer-0

[18] "His Kampf: Richard Spencer is a troll and an icon for white supremacists. He is also my high-school classmate," Graeme Wood, *The Atlantic*, June 2017, p. 16

America is responsible as a nation for the creation and continuation of an increasingly hostile country in which race defines who we are. In this country, the media, the poverty pimps, and the politicians all traffic in race. Racial trafficking is increasingly becoming as American as motherhood and apple pie. Misconceptions are now considered facts, and the American soul continues to be hollow. Race is a national security issue that harms America as much as foreign wars do.

Politicians pledge to protect America from all enemies foreign and domestic. Why then are they not protecting us from the enemy that is race? It is because they profit from trafficking in it. As they always do, they put their interests first until it is no longer politically expedient to do so. Too many Americans are simply willing participants in this racial imbroglio that will ultimately blow a hole in what is left of America's racial soul.

Plank Number One: BLM Supporters Advocate Only for Blacks

Black Lives Matter has been viewed by many to mean that *only* black lives matter. This can be seen in the development of the alternate hashtags "#AllLivesMatter" and "#BlueLivesMatter" and by the activist group White Lives Matter. Though BLM has clearly said in its mission statement that its goal is to end the marginalization of African-Americans, there are many who believe that the real purpose is to sow division and dissension. Have they sown division? Or was the division already there and BLM is being blamed for it? It is a bit of both.

First, given the deep racial cesspool that is America, saying that BLM sows racial division is not unexpected. Second, if the racial division did not exist, how could they sow it? Third, what evidence shows that they have sown division? Finally, I am no fan of BLM. I find its approach to be juvenile, not well thought out, and simply self-serving.

In my view, BLM's approach seems to be warmed-over protests with no real objective. It is often unclear to me what adherents gain from their rallies and other gatherings and what meaningful change they have made.

But that's the problem with reactionary movements: they are reacting to something, and so they are defined by the need to react. Surely, white supremacy is nothing new. The National Association for the Advancement of Colored People was started in part with the objective of eradicating racism. However, it has morphed into an unwieldy institution beholden to the political left.

BLM risks being a fad if it simply reacts to white supremacy writ large. Its alignment with the political left also carries huge risks. Issues of race and racism in modern-day America will not be solved simply by protests, phraseology, and shouting. Instead, those issues require sustained actions across the political spectrum. The issue is not simply the existence of the alt-right, it is ensuring that what members of the alt-right stand for does not become entrenched in America's soul.

A poll conducted on race relations in September 2015 by the Marist Institute for Public Opinion found that 42 percent of white Americans are unsure or do not have an opinion about Black Lives Matter, and 41 percent think that Black Lives Matter advocates violence.[19] A Harvard-Harris poll conducted in July 2017 found that 57 percent of those polled have an unfavorable view of BLM and 62 percent believe that the focus on police behavior has handcuffed law enforcement officials.[20] To be sure, issues of police brutality affecting black men in the United States is real. While BLM has brought this issue forward, it has not sufficiently

---

[19] "PBS NewsHour/Marist Poll Summary of National Findings," Marist College Institute for Public Opinion, Sept. 2015, retrieved July 14, 2016, http://maristpoll.marist.edu/npr-pbs-newshour-marist-poll-results-september-2018

[20] "Poll: 57 percent have negative view of Black Lives Matter movement," Jonathan Easley, The Hill, Aug. 2, 2017, retrieved Aug. 18, 2017, https://thehill.com/homenews/campaign/344985-poll-57-percent-have-negative-view-of-black-lives-matter-movement

addressed how to solve this issue by working with the police. Instead, its widespread painting of police as the enemy has caused backlash.

I am not suggesting that there are police officers who are not complicit in crimes against black men. I am saying that they, too, have to be part of the solution. The current tactics BLM adherents use have not resulted in any meaningful change. Instead, they have resulted in the alienation of law enforcement and have created further division.

Plank Number Two: BLM Supporters Are Racists and Want Everything to Be About Race

Since its inception, BLM has been accused of propagating racism. Any attention and focus on ways minorities have been treated differently in this country have been met by attempts to not acknowledge them or to deflect attention towards some additional problem. This is readily seen in the #AllLivesMatter movement, which seeks to rally people around the fact that everyone is equal and should be treated equally in this country, but which of course refuses to acknowledge that BLM was created expressly to bring attention to the disparities in treatment of blacks within the legal system.

The fundamental problem I have with All Lives Matter is the same problem I have with BLM. They are both trapped in backlash politics. That is, both groups react to the enduring badges and incidents of racism not with substantive approaches but with inflammatory discourse intended to gin up support for their causes without any discernible change or measurable outcomes.

According to the Southern Poverty Law Center, Black Lives Matter is not a hate group. But as its president, J. Richard Cohen, states, "The perception that it is racist illustrates the problem. Our society as a whole still does not accept that racial injustice remains pervasive. And, unfortunately, the fact that white people tend to see race as a zero-sum game may actually impede progress."[21]

Plank Number Three: BLM Supporters Don't Want to Acknowledge or Work to Redress Other Issues Facing the Black Community

Another way BLM detracters try to deflect from the stated mission of the group is to bring up the issue of black-on-black crime. They state that the group should be addressing that issue, as it is more prevalent, without realizing that there are already initiatives that exist to address those issues within the black community. Why does BLM have to address that as well? The 2017 Harvard-Harris survey found that 70 percent of respondents believe that black people committing crimes against other black people is a bigger problem than police violence.

The movement does not need to address every issue in the lives of black people. However, it has branded itself as an organization that focuses on making sure that the lives of blacks matter. Its members have a focus and a mission, and they are taking on the issue that is most salient to them. If people want to know where the conversations about black-on-black crime are happening, they are happening in the neighborhoods where violence is dominating the streets. Stop the Violence marches, Scared Straight programs, gang counseling, neighborhood watches, and the like are all indicators that the community is trying to deal with the violence within it.

Data from the FBI's Uniform Crime Reporting Program found that in 2016, 83.5 percent of whites were killed by other whites, compared to 90.1 percent of blacks killed by other blacks, yet there is no national outcry to discuss white-on-white violence.[22]

---

[21] "Black Lives Matter is Not a Hate Group," J. Richard Cohen, *Time*, July 19, 2016

[22] "Crime in the United States: Arrests 2013," FBI: UCR, Department of Justice, Federal Bureau of Investigation, Criminal Justice Information Services Division, https://ucr.fbi.gov/crime-in-the-u.s/2013/crime-in-the-u.s.-2013

Plank Number Four: BLM Supporters' Tactics Are Disturbing, and They Believe in a Mob Mentality that Incites Violence

They are shutting down freeways, disrupting community meetings,[23] and confronting politicians. In 2015, they rushed to the stage and disrupted a Martin O'Malley and Bernie Sanders rally to ask the candidates their views on police violence.[24] They have organized protests around the deaths of African-American men and women at the hands of the police since 2014, and organized marches for transgender women and rallies around the anniversaries of the deaths of Freddie Gray and Trayvon Martin, to name a few. They have never advocated for violence and have denounced violence toward law enforcement.

Heidi Beirich, the head of the Southern Poverty Law Center's Intelligence Project, states that Black Lives Matter is not considered a hate group. She says,

"Black Lives Matter is not a racist group; anyone can join. It's a movement to expand civil rights for the oppressed in this society. It's a peaceful protest against oppression. There's simply no equivalence between Black Lives Matter and a hate group. It's truly offensive to equate them."[25]

The policy of nonviolence is shared by BLM activists around the country. "I refuse to cede the moral high ground to the supremacy we fight," says Brittany Packnett, an activist and the cofounder of Campaign Zero, which aims to end police violence. "We don't need to

---

[23] "How Black Lives Matter became a thorn in the side of L.A. leaders," Shelby Grad, *Los Angeles Times*, Oct. 20, 2015

[24] "Protesters drove Bernie Sanders from one Seattle stage. At his next stop, 15,000 people showed," John Wagner, *Washington Post*, Aug. 8, 2015

[25] "A Year Inside the Black Lives Matter Movement: How America's new generation of civil rights activists is mobilizing in the age of Trump," Touré, *Rolling Stone*, Dec. 7, 2017, https://www.rollingstone.com/politics/politics-news/a-year-inside-the-black-lives-matter-movement-204982/

become that which we are fighting." History has shown that violence inevitably occurs when the status quo—especially regarding race—is challenged.[26] The Southern Poverty Law Center has spoken and continues to speak on these issues. However, the reality is that its members need to disclose and not hide the fact that their allegiance is to white liberal policies. The failure to disclose this allegiance, in my view, taints any claims of complete objectivity.

The Alt-Right

Let's get this straight. The alt-right is not mainstream Conservatism. It is not even mainstream Libertarian or mainstream Republican. Instead, it is a group of racists—vanquished hoodlums who have ditched the hoods in favor of the bowels of the internet, where they ferment hate and spew venom.

The alt-right does not seem to have the same problem with misperceptions as BLM. Its members are proud of their ideals and don't see anything wrong with the violence that is carried out by followers of their tenets. They advocate for white supremacy, anti-Semitism, misogyny, homophobia, racism, and Islamophobia, to name a few beliefs. Organizations espousing alt-right beliefs feel they are right to believe these things, thus there is no reason to hide their nature. Unless you are white, Christian, heterosexual, and (probably) male, you are inferior. Those who profess alt-right tendencies regularly state these sentiments online. Lone white gunmen, including William Atchison, Dylann Roof, Nikolas Cruz, and James Fields Jr., who have perpetrated multiple attacks, have championed alt-right beliefs in their young lives. They believe the world would be a better place without those "others" who commit crimes, take jobs, and are terrorists.

---

[26] "Don't criticize Black Lives Matter for provoking violence. The civil rights movement did, too," Sebastian, Simone, *Washington Post*, Oct. 1, 2015

Those who think that the alt-right appeared simply as a fringe group with a radical ideology are either completely stupid or have an uncomfortable relationship with the truth. The alt-right is a reaction to one of the most recent political movements: the election of Barack Obama as president. It is also a reaction to what its loyalists see as political correctness and diversity and inclusion run amok. Members believe that "niggers" have gained too much and that America has lost its soul.

Even worse, in their view, uppity "niggers" such as Obama have no place in the white man's house. Although so many of their members see technology as evil, technology has replaced the white sheet of the Ku Klux Klan as their weapon of mass destruction. They use the internet to gather virtually and to meet up in person, to spew hate, and to grow their membership.

To be sure, the alt-right is buttressed in its beliefs by Thomas Jefferson, who mused (in his book *Notes on the State of Virginia*) that the Negro simply does not have the capacity to reason and think critically. This rationale occurred just as modernity was on the upswing. Thus, the alt-right has ridden that wave. The most sinister and vilest aspects of modernity provide material support for the alt-right. Members lay bare the reality that modern Western civilization codified elements of white supremacy upon which the republic was built and still stands. The alt-right is not about a movement, by nature of its stranglehold on white supremacy; whiteness does not require a movement. Instead, it is an ideology that is in the blood of a modern America.

We cannot escape the fact that we live in a global world defined, controlled, manipulated, and, in many cases, led by the internet. According to author Rachel Holmes:

"In an increasingly online everyday life, our use of social media has become a medium for normalising the acceptability of intrusion

and behavioural correction. We are bombarded by "helpful recom-mendations" on education, health, relationships, taxes and leisure matched to our tracked user profiles that nudge us towards prod-ucts and services to make us better citizen consumers. The app told you that you only took 100 steps today. The ad for the running shoes will arrive tomorrow.

We risk allowing ourselves to become a vast network of informants on each other and ourselves. Think about GPS-based location tracking on your mobile phone; think about social media apps where we broadcast our spontaneous thoughts, social lives and relationships."[27]

It would be easy to simply dismiss the alt-right as a bunch of losers living in the basements of their parents' homes, and for whom life is a miserable stew brought on by "niggers," "coons," "spics," "Jews," "wetbacks," and "Orientals." To do so, however, is incred-ibly naive. Richard Spencer realizes the need to ensure that white supremacy does not die. He also realizes that college campuses are fertile ground for budding white supremacists. He told *Mother Jones*, "I do think you need to get them while they are young" and, "People in college are at this point in their lives where they are actually open to alternative perspectives...."[28]

Despite all of the attempts to cloak alt-right supporters in legit-imate clothing, the reality is that they have committed and continue to commit unspeakable crimes in the name of white supremacy. Here is just a sampling of crimes committed by those loyal to the alt-right:

---

[27] "We Let Technology into Our Lives. And Now It's Starting to Control Us," Rachel Holmes, *The Guardian*, Nov. 28, 2016, https://www.theguardian.com/commentisfree/2016/nov/28/technology-our-lives-control-us-internet-giants-data

[28] 'The Push to Enlist 'Alt-Right' Recruits on College Campuses," Josh Harkinson, MotherJones.com, Dec. 6, 2016

Hate crimes attributed to the alt-right
• A 58-year-old African American man in Scottsdale, Arizona, says a white neighbor yelled racial slurs while stabbing him three times with a knife. Police say the attacker showed signs of mental illness. The victim insists the attack was a hate crime, but Arizona doesn't have a state hate crime law.
• Two middle-school teachers were attacked in the bathroom of a Sacramento, California, bar. One of the victims said the assault happened after he was overheard talking to his boyfriend on the phone. The attacker reportedly called the teachers names during the assault and law enforcement officials have classified the assault as a hate crime. A crowdfunding campaign for one of the victims, who suffered serious damage to his eye, has raised over $10,000.
• A transgender student at De Anza College in Cupertino, California, was reportedly assaulted two times in the same parking garage in the span of a week. The suspect yelled an anti-gay slur during the second attack. The victim was unable to determine if the same perpetrator was responsible for both beatings.
• Police arrested a trio of North Carolina teens for a multistate vandalism spree. They allegedly blew up a mailbox with a homemade explosive device, slashed tires on cars, spray-painted an upside-down cross on a church van and scrawled swastikas on several vehicles. "These individuals have no respect and regard for anyone's personal property not even a place of worship. This will not be tolerated," Madison County Sheriff J.E. Harwood told Fox Carolina.
• Students and community members at an upstate New York high school were barraged with harassment after Breitbart,, The Daily Stormer and 4chan latched on to a controversy over the race of an actor cast in a production of "The Hunchback of Notre Dame." The show was canceled when a white student was selected for a role that, in the Disney film, was depicted with brown skin. As The New York Times reported, students were sent pictures of swastikas drawn over their faces and one parent discovered her family's (inaccurate) personal information posted online.

Source: "The Hate Report: 43 Alt-Right Murders in Four Years," by Will Carless and Aaron Sankin, published by Reveal, *Feb. 9, 2018.* [29]

Is There a Connection Between the Alt-Right and BLM?

Can one credibly make a comparison between the alt-right and BLM? I don't think so. The alt-right is steeped in a white supremacy-fed ideology, and BLM is a reaction to that ideology.

Black Lives Matter is an organization and a movement trying to remind people that this country cannot and should not demarginalize

---

[29] "The Hate Report: 43 Alt-Right Murders in Four Years," Will Carless and Aaron Sankin, *Reveal*, Feb. 9, 2018, https://www.revealnews.org/blog/the-hate-report-43-alt-right-murders-in -four-years/

a segment of the population because of skin color. That black lives do matter just as white lives, Asian lives, Latino lives, female lives, LGBTQI+ lives, Christian lives, Jewish lives, and so on matter. Supporters recognize that there are many issues which impact the full inclusion into American society of people of color. One issue highlights the impact that flawed policy can have and has had on the African-American community.

They also recognize that it is almost impossible to move forward as a country without understanding how policies formed to marginalize any group—in this case especially, blacks—negatively impact society.

The alt-right is a collection of different organizations espousing the same or similar beliefs, including white supremacy, neo-Confederacy, neo-Nazism, fascism, and hatred for Islam, women, and the LGBTQ community, among others. The alt-right is actively working to divide the country, get rid of democracy, and "do something" about the "others" who don't look or act like them. Their tactics can be described only as "by any means necessary," and it has been reported that individuals influenced by the alt-right have been responsible for the deaths and injuries of more than a hundred people since 2014.[30] There is no cohesion to the alt-right, as it is not a movement but a collection of ideologies that show disdain and hatred for anyone who is not white, male, heterosexual, or Christian. With so many groups advocating for similar ideas, it allows those following the ideology to (publicly) disavow the actions of those perceived to be particularly abhorrent.

Richard Spencer, one of the more recognized "leaders" of the alt-right, has stated that the Nazis were violent, and:

"that is not something that I would have anything to do with. I've never advocated that or ever glorified that. I am a dissident

---

[30] "The Alt-Right is Killing People," Southern Poverty Law Center, Feb. 5, 2018, https://www.splcenter.org/20180205/alt-right-killing-people

intellectual. I am not in charge of the police force or the Army. I'm not ordering the roundup of anyone and throwing them into camps."[31]

A comparison between BLM and the alt-right is impossible, because they are not remotely similar entities. At the heart of BLM are anger, fear, mistrust, and resignation, wrapped up in the hope and belief that change can come about, and that this land its supporters call home can finally be a place where they belong, along with their fellow citizens of any race. It is a message of wanting to be included. In stark contrast, at the heart of the alt-right are anger, fear, mistrust, and the hope that one day whiteness will return to reign supreme and nonwhites will simply return to their nonhuman, subservient roles in what is properly a white universe.

At the beginning of this chapter, I mentioned that BLM and the alt-right are viewed as being on opposite sides of a spectrum. The question becomes, what are the end points of the spectrum, or what does the spectrum measure? For many people, it appears that the spectrum is black supremacy versus white supremacy. Many people don't like BLM because they believe BLM is trying to push black people forward to the detriment of all other people. There is a sense of unease among white people that they are falling behind in an increasingly diverse country and world.

A study by two prominent psychologists found that white people believe *decreases* in perceived bias against black people are associated with *increases* in perceived bias against white people—and that whites view anti-white bias as a bigger societal problem than anti-black bias. The psychologists also found that blacks do not believe that racism is a zero-sum game; blacks feel that rights can accommodate everyone and

---

[31] "His Kampf: Richard Spencer is a troll and an icon for white supremacists. He is also my high-school classmate," Graeme Wood, *The Atlantic*, June 2017

should apply to everyone.[32] What if the spectrum were instead based on social justice or the equality of citizens under the law ("We hold these truths to be self-evident, that all men are created equal")? Then on the one side (not even on the end, but close to it), we have Black Lives Matter's stated goal of seeking to ensure that a group of citizens in this country is treated equally under the law (and, by extension, all are being treated equally under the law) and the alt-right seeking to uphold the supremacy of the white race, believing that equality is only for those who are white. This country has spent its existence trying to live up to the values laid out in the Declaration of Independence and the Constitution. It has been a bloody, painful, heart-wrenching, torturous journey for everyone.

The existence of both these groups shows us that division along racial and ideological lines is fast becoming the rule and not the exception in an America populated by enemies from within. Yet we are doing very little about it. Instead of we the people trying to solve the issue, we are looking to a dysfunctional government that relies on division to win elections. We revel in activities such as training sessions that help us address "unconscious bias," and we move further right or further left on the political spectrum.

To be sure, there are police officers who make arrests solely on the basis of race, and for that they should be tried and, if the evidence bears it out, convicted and jailed. Police officers have to realize that you cannot simply arrest your way out of crime. BLM and the police are in defensive mode. BLM is trying to stay true to its stated mission, and the police officers are trying to defend their departments against charges of racism and discrimination. This has resulted in a zero-sum game that further chips away at America's soul while continuing the division.

---

[32] "Whites See Racism as a Zero-Sum Game That They Are Now Losing," Michael Norton and Samuel R. Sommers, *Perspectives on Psychological Science* (2011) 6: 215

It seems to me that we are headed for a civil war in the streets of America unlike anything we have ever seen before, unless we stop the self-segregation, the penchant to rely exclusively on government to solve this problem, failing to hold government responsible for anything, and understanding and learning history and why we are so bitterly divided. Following this path of normalizing white supremacy and creating a divisive and hollow response to it mean that we surrender America and sink into the base and vile abyss that will consume America's soul. Some will say that maybe civil war is the answer, since it would resolve the issues once and for all. To them, I say the Civil War was one of the most brutal and consequential wars in American history. More Americans died in that war than in all other wars combined. The nation fought against itself and was torn asunder.

CHAPTER 8

Originalism:
The Battle Hymn of the Republic

T he Supreme Court of the United States (SCOTUS) affects the lives of every person living in this country. The court has one duty and one duty only: to interpret the Constitution of the United States. So how does the court see itself? According to www.supremecourt.gov:

> *"The Constitution of the United States is a carefully balanced document. It is designed to provide for a national government sufficiently strong and flexible to meet the needs of the republic, yet sufficiently limited and just to protect the guaranteed rights of citizens; it permits a balance between society's need for order and the individual's right to freedom. To assure these ends, the Framers of the Constitution created three independent and coequal branches of government. That this Constitution has provided continuous democratic government through the periodic stresses of more than*

two centuries illustrates the genius of the American system of government.

The complex role of the Supreme Court in this system derives from its authority to invalidate legislation or executive actions which, in the Court's considered judgment, conflict with the Constitution. This power of "judicial review" has given the Court a crucial responsibility in assuring individual rights, as well as in maintaining a "living Constitution" whose broad provisions are continually applied to complicated new situations."[1]

In America, we live or die by the Constitution. Over the years, the court has moved from being an objective and disinterested interpreter of the law to being a highly partisan body that makes the law based on its conservative or liberal ideology. The court has become yet another entity in a deeply divided America.

Simply look at the process by which a Supreme Court justice is appointed. The president announces his pick, then people from both political parties begin the pitch to define the nominee in the court of public opinion. The rush to define the nominee is done so that the parties can score political points and get ahead of the message, leading to victory. But victory for whom? And how do we define "victory"?

The issue is the strict interpretation of the Constitution. There can be no victory without jurists who understand this and conduct themselves accordingly.

Yes, the Constitution was written before modern times, and no, I am not suggesting that we go back to a time when women were barefoot and pregnant and blacks were slaves. In fact, in considering whether Negroes might have standing to sue in United States courts, or whether slave property might be afforded less protection than any other kind of property, the chief justice wrote:

---

[1] "The Court and Constitutional Interpretation," https://www.supremecourt.gov/about/constitutional.aspx

"No one, we presume, supposes that any change in public opinion or feeling, in relation to this unfortunate race, in the civilized nations of Europe or in this country, should induce the court to give to the words of the Constitution a more liberal construction in their favor than they were intended to bear when the instrument was framed and adopted. Such an argument would be altogether inadmissible in any tribunal called on to interpret it. If any of its provisions are deemed unjust, there is a mode prescribed in the instrument itself by which it may be amended; but while it remains unaltered, it must be construed now as it was understood at the time of its adoption. It is not only the same in words, but the same in meaning, and delegates the same powers to the Government, and reserves and secures the same rights and privileges to the citizen; and as long as it continues to exist in its present form, it speaks not only in the same words, but with the same meaning and intent with which it spoke when it came from the hands of its framers, and was voted on and adopted by the people of the United States. Any other rule of construction would abrogate the judicial character of this court, and make it the mere reflex of the popular opinion or passion of the day. This court was not created by the Constitution for such purposes."[2]

How soon we forget that the republic nearly ended, due to a rancorous and deep-seated dispute over the institution of slavery, careening into a civil war a century and a half ago. In 1856, violence over slavery erupted in the august chamber of the U.S. Senate, when an antislavery lawmaker from Massachusetts, Charles Sumner, was caned on the Senate floor by a member of the House from South Carolina, Preston Brooks. We don't want to return to those days.

---

[2] *Dred Scott v. John F. A. Sandford*, 60 U.S. (19 How.) 393 (1857), https://scholar.google.com/scholar_case?case=3231372247892780026&q=Scott+v.+Sandford&hl=en&as_sdt=6,43&as_vis=1

I am arguing for a return to sanity and a SCOTUS that interprets rather than makes law. Leave the lawmaking to elected officials. By having a Supreme Court in which originalism prevails, we will get closer and closer to healing the divide. The Constitution is a well-thought-out and interrelated document, with subtle balances incorporated throughout. Reflecting the founders' understanding of the self-motivated impulses of human nature, the Constitution erected devices that work to frustrate those impulses while leaving open channels for effective and mutually supportive collaboration.

SCOTUS has a role to play in healing that divide, as it chooses those cases it wants to hear every term. A review of the cases it chooses reveals that the issues presented are, in fact, many of the issues that are at the heart of a deeply divided America. The issues can be resolved only when the Supreme Court returns to simply applying the Constitution instead of twisting its meaning so badly that one can barely recognize it. The modern-day court applies a rather fluid approach to the Constitution. Some claim that the justices are "strict constructionists," in the vein of Thomas Jefferson.

An Originalist View of the Constitution

Ours is a written constitution. So it is purely logical to expect that all branches of government with jurisdiction over the laws have the meaning of the Constitution as their foundation. If they do not, then how can we expect that their decisions are in line with the Constitution? The short answer is that we cannot. The failure to have an original view and understanding of the Constitution has allowed and in fact encouraged political intervention in the process of selecting and appointing justices to the Supreme Court. Congress now wants to know how justices would rule on specific topics. Of course, justices are lifetime appointees and rule however they damn well please.

In recent years, the originalist view has gone the way of the horse and buggy and has been replaced by a "living, breathing document" view. This suggests that the Constitution is a flexible political document, the interpretation of which changes with the party in power. This has simply led to a more divided America. Let us examine recent cases before the court for an explanation.

Masterpiece Cakeshop, Ltd. v. Colorado Civil Rights Commission (decided June 4, 2018)

In *Masterpiece Cakeshop*, the justices were tasked with deciding if Colorado's public accommodations law violated the First Amendment religious rights of a cake maker who declined to make a cake for a same-sex marriage event. Instead, the ruling focused on the conduct of the Colorado Rights Commission in its initial decision in the case. Here, the court did not rule on the substance of the case but instead focused on the way the commission decided the case.

In the seven-to-two decision, Justice Anthony Kennedy said that the commission incorrectly acted in its decision that Masterpiece Cakeshop had violated the Colorado Anti-Discrimination Act (CADA). Kennedy said the baker, Jack Phillips, was "entitled to a neutral and respectful consideration of his claims in all the circumstances of the case,"[3] but the statements of some commission officials cast doubts on the neutrality of their decision.

"That consideration was compromised, however, by the Commission's treatment of Phillips' case, which showed elements of a clear and impermissible hostility toward the sincere religious beliefs motivating his objection," Kennedy said. For those and other reasons, Kennedy said, "the Commission's treatment of Phillips's case violated the State's

---

[3] *Masterpiece Cakeshop Ltd. v. Colorado Civil Rights Commission*, 584 U.S. (2018), https://supreme.justia.com/cases/federal/us/584/16-111/

duty under the First Amendment not to base laws or regulations on hostility to a religion or religious viewpoint."

This was an originalist decision.

First, as the opinion instructs, among the questions raised by this case is whether what the couple asked for—a cake for a private celebration—is really "speech" or "free exercise of religion" at all.

Second, the record developed in the court below failed to provide sufficient facts to answer a crucial question, which is whether Phillips refused only to bake a cake with a wedding message or refused to provide any cake at all for Charlie Craig and Dave Mullins's celebration.

Third, as in any purely constitutional decision, the court got it right in looking closely at the fact that the facts in question occurred before the court's decision, in *Obergefell v. Hodges*,[4] that same-sex couples have a right to marry. Thus, Phillips in part based his denial on the fact that, at the time, Colorado did not permit same-sex marriages—that "the potential customers 'were doing something illegal.'"

Fourth, as Justice Kennedy pointed out during oral argument, the record was muddled by antireligious statements made by state officials who considered the case below.

So that we are all clear, originalism, properly understood and applied, leads to a less divided America because of the fundamental nature of its principles. Few will disagree that the Constitution is the document which has stopped this nation from becoming a lawless enclave of robber barons. Originalism is the frame of reference and tool of interpretation, the glue that holds us together. It is crucial in part because it is completely and unequivocally in sync with the sum and substance of the U.S. Constitution, which restricts, limits, and

---

[4] *Obergefell et al. v. Hodges, Director, Ohio Department of Health, et al.*, Supreme Court of the United States, October Term 2014. https://www.supremecourt.gov/opinions/14pdf/14-556_3204.pdf

ensures that the courts do not contravene the Constitution by making decisions that swing with the politics of the times.

The framers of the Constitution of 1787 could not predict the future, but they correctly concluded that there was a need to form and live up to an enduring government, for "ourselves and our Posterity." The phrase "we the people" is bandied about as if the framers were thinking simply about a random collection of people who would get together for a coffee klatch. Given the work of the founders to establish the Constitution and include the preamble stating "we the people," it would be illogical to conclude that they were merely talking about individuals who were coming together for a single event. Instead, the framers were founding a nation, a country, and a government that would endure and withstand the test of time. Thus, they envisaged a country in which all people would come together for the good of the republic.

Regardless of whether they intended it or not, the framers were not only building a nation, they were building a generation. They knew that America would change over time, that decisions would have to be made across generations, and that tough calls would have to be made. And so they planned that we the people would come together to do so. But this means that decisions would have to be made with originalism as the key ingredient. Had they wanted a "living, breathing document," they would have made it easier to simply amend the Constitution.

The framers were clear in their intent. I find it incredible that people refuse to see how originalism is consistent with our constitutional republic. The framers were clear that government is accountable fully to us, "the people." What this means is that the people, and not the government, control our own destinies.

The "Living, Breathing Document" Approach to the Constitution

Yet far too many courts are deciding cases based on the idea that the Constitution is alive. The late justice Antonin Scalia was right:

> *"Most American courts today rule by a 'living constitution' idea: that the constitution should be interpreted in accordance with the times, taking on new meaning based on each generation's understanding.... But this principle threatens American democracy by affording too much power to the Supreme Court."*[5]

Originalism is so foundational to our founding as a country and to what we have accomplished as a nation, yet a liberal view would have us forget all we know and get rid of originalism because it does not fit the mode of liberalism. If we did that, where would we be as a nation? We would be in a space where the framers and their original intent mean nothing. The Constitution would be open to changing without amendment and by unelected judges and partisan lawmakers. Thus, feelings, politics, and partisanship, like a wolf dressed in sheep's clothing, would prevail. Government would no longer exist to guard our liberty. Instead, it would exist to run our lives. We would become accountable to government and not the other way around. This, however, is partisanship and not law.

And we have begun to see this with the courts in recent years. Obamacare stands out as a glaring example. This bill was not about healthcare; it was about raising taxes. However, to avoid being accused of raising taxes, which would have been political suicide, the Obama administration spun this as a healthcare bill:

---

[5] "Supreme Court Justice Antonin Scalia rejects idea of 'Living Constitution,'" Alice Su, *The Times of Trenton*, https://www.nj.com/mercer/index.ssf/2012/12/supreme_court_justice_antonin.html

"Rather than operating as a tax on income, the mandate is a tax on the person and is, therefore, a capitation tax. Therefore, the 16th Amendment's grant of power to Congress to assess an income tax does not apply. The Constitution does allow Congress to assess a capitation tax, but that requires the tax be assessed evenly based on population. That is not how the Obamacare mandate works. It exempts and carves out far too many exceptions to pass muster as a capitation tax."[6]

What liberals simply refuse to accept about originalism is that it is not simply and uncritically justified by history. Moreover, it in and of itself does not require an unequivocal need for over-interpretation. Words have natural and original meaning. The right to bear and keep arms, in an originalist view, is deeply rooted in citizen power and federal government checks and balances. The framers realized that if the right to bear arms were eliminated, only the federal government would have arms.

Janus v. AFSCME was correctly decided. As Justice Samuel Alito states in the court's opinion, "Forcing free and independent individuals to endorse ideas they find objectionable is always demeaning."[7]

Unions have had untold sway over their members for the longest period of time. The primary tool they have used has been dues for members and nonmembers alike. More important, they have used those funds and the labor of their members to give generously to liberal elected officials and liberal causes. In far too many cases, both members and nonmembers have not agreed with the political causes. Janus has shaken the once solid political ground from underneath the unions. Public sector unions have always relied on dues to

[6] "White House Admits ObamaCare's Individual Mandate Is a Tax," Conn Carroll, *The Heritage Foundation Commentary on Health Care Reform*, July 26, 2010, https://www.heritage.org/health-care-reform/commentary/white-house-admits-obamacares-individual-mandate-tax

[7] *Janus v. American Federation of State, County, and Municipal Employees*, Council 31, et al., decided June 27, 2018, https://www.supremecourt.gov/opinions/17pdf/16-1466_2b3j.pdf

support their activities including political activity. Before Janus, it was a long-standing practice to collect dues from employees regardless of whether or not they were union members. Of course, many employees were livid about this practice. First, they never signed up to be union members and thus felt that the dues were un unfair "tax" or "burden" on them. Second, the unions gave mostly to the Democrats and not all employees were Democrats and so many felt that the unions had a political sway using their money that they simply had not consented to.

The court was unequivocal in its opinion. The practice has to end. Should the union desire to collect dues from non-members, those members had to consent prior to the collection of said dues. In common Labor Law parlance, the employees had to "opt in" or give prior written consent.

Unions and their supporters blasted the Court's decision in Janus on the grounds that it was an ideological one and not an originalist one. In other words they claimed that the Court was simply using right wing ideology to justify its decision. The problem with this argument is that they offered no evidence for their claim. Instead, they chose to use vitriol and hyperbole. An originalist understanding of the constitution is simple really. Decide the cases based on the way the document is written. It is not any more complicated than that. To help understand originalism more, I now analyze some of the words of Samuel Adams, one of the Founding Fathers. His words provide both color and context to the arguments surrounding originalism.

* * * * *

As Samuel Adams wrote, "That in all free States the Constitution is fixed; & as the supreme Legislative derives its Power & Authority from the Constitution, it cannot overleap the Bounds of it without destroying its own foundation."[8]

Government and its sprawling power were never contemplated by the Constitution. But as the courts became more political and the shift away from originalism became a way of life, government began to take over our lives. We have moved from limited government to limitless government. If we understand anything about originalism, we understand that the Constitution is the basis for the existence of several branches of the federal government. However, the move to the nonsensical view of "living, breathing" has turned this form of interpretation on its head, with agency heads in several branches of government believing that the Constitution is incidental and not plenary to their existence.

The seminal case of *Marbury v. Madison*, which I use to teach my constitutional law class, is all we need to know about the framers and the Constitution:

> *"[I]t follows that originalism limits the judiciary. It prevents the Supreme Court from asserting its will over the careful mix of institutional arrangements that are charged with making policy, each accountable in various ways to the people. Chief Justice John Marshall, overtly deferring to the intention of the Framers, insisted "that the framers of the constitution contemplated that instrument, as a rule for the government of courts, as well as of the legislature." In words that judges and academics might well contemplate today, Marshall said, "Why otherwise does it direct the judges to take an oath to support it? This oath certainly applies, in an especial manner, to their conduct in their official character. How immoral to impose it on them, if they were to be used as the instruments, and*

---

the knowing instruments, for violating what they swear to support!"
(Marbury v. Madison)[9]

Anti-Federalists were unrelenting in their views that the freedoms of speech and press were the sharpest and most deeply cutting tools against the evil of tyranny, and that exercise of those rights was necessary to control and limit government.[10]

The freedoms of speech and press were seen as the essence of free government, through which people could be free to limit government by political means.[11]

The Illogical Liberal and the Constitution

In writing this chapter, I harked back to my days as a first-year law student and how deeply I revered the Constitution. First, I realized that it is not a perfect document, but nonetheless, it is an incredible document that spells out enumerated powers with ease. Second, I recall how many of my fellow students gravitated to a much different view of the Constitution than I did. Many of them saw the document as one that was outdated and had outlived its time. I took the position that the Constitution had stood the test of time.

Liberals stand in the way of the courts' helping to heal a divided government because of their nonsensical belief that Congress is inherently all-powerful. A simple reading and understanding of documents and papers that led to the forming of the union reveals otherwise.

---

[9] "The Originalist Perspective," David F. Forte, T*he Heritage Guide to the Constitution*, https://www.heritage.org/constitution/#!/introessays/3

[10] Letters of Centinel No. 2, in 2 *The Complete Anti-Federalist*, Herbert J. Storing ed., 1981, pp 143-144; also Speech of Patrick Henry in Virginia Ratifying Convention in 3 *The Debates in the Several State Conventions on the Adoption of the Federal Constitution* (1836), Jonathan Elliott ed., 2d Ed., p 449

[11] "Report on the Virginia Resolutions" (Jan. 1800), James Madison, reprinted in 5 *The Founders' Constitution*, Philip B. Kurland and Ralph Lerner eds., 1987, p 145

The Constitution granted Congress a finite list of enumerated powers. And therein lies liberals' inherent animosity toward the document: it limits their ability to wreak havoc on the nation through the flawed, self-destructive, corrupt, out-of-control institution that is posing as Congress. It is the Constitution that wields power, not an elite bunch of egotistical swamp dwellers. Liberals live under the misguided and delusional belief that it is government and government alone that can build the perfect society. They have attempted to take the courts away from originalism because they know that an originalist view of the Constitution simply does not allow this to happen. They have begun to lose both the battle and the war.

Conservatives are realistic in our approach that the Constitution is a constraining document designed to avoid tyranny. We understand that human beings are, by nature, about themselves and their beliefs. Thus, the Constitution exists to check this behavior. If we accept the liberal view, we would simply get rid of the Constitution and replace it with government at large. Liberals seem to forget that Americans cannot stand being governed without our consenting to that. The purpose of our national government is not to take over our lives. It is to handle those national affairs we think need to be managed, but only with our consent.

In fact, the federal government created by the Constitutional Convention resembles nothing like the sprawling, slow-moving, paper-pushing one we have today. It is clear that Congress has very limited powers and that they are specified in Article I, Section 8. All other powers are reserved for the states and the people. However, the courts have strayed from originalist orthodoxy during liberal control and have now made central government much more powerful than was intended. Thus, we find ourselves in the position of the courts' effectively amending the Constitution without the people's having voted through the process provided by the Constitution. No wonder division runs rampant.

Why the Travel Ban Case Matters

One of the most significant cases of the 2017–2018 SCOTUS term was the so-called travel ban case. By a five-to-four vote, the Supreme Court issued a decision in *Trump v. Hawaii*, upholding the travel ban.

The Politics of the Travel Ban Case

As a presidential candidate, Donald Trump made it clear that he thought there were too many people coming to America who had a hatred for America, and that he wanted them banned from traveling here because they made the country less safe. In a statement titled "Preventing Muslim Immigration," the GOP presidential front-runner said all Muslims should be barred until "our country's representatives can figure out what's going on."

Once elected president, he realized that enacting the ban was not as easy as he'd thought. In fact, the attorneys general of several liberal-leaning states fought vigorously to defeat the first, second, and third versions of the ban, with several lower courts striking it down and others upholding it. The president and his staff drafted three versions of the ban, with version three finally being upheld, as it was more narrowly tailored and complied with the plenary power of the president on issues of national security.

Democrats were livid when the court upheld the final version of the ban. They were powerless in both Congress and the courts to do anything about it. As Dick Durbin, the Senate's number-two Democrat, told CNN:

> *"I think it's clear that the history of this travel ban is one that is not to the credit of the United States. First, the President came out with a travel ban, which had to be rewritten at least one time, maybe twice, and the net result of it sadly was to suggest that when it came to countries with large Muslim populations, they weren't welcome*

in the United States.... We need to keep out every dangerous person who tries to come in this country, but to categorically brand people because of their religion or their background or country they're from is just not the way we should do things in America."[12]

The Ban

Under the ban, President Donald Trump, using his express authority, suspended, at least temporarily, the admission of individuals from seven countries—Syria, Iran, Libya, Yemen, Somalia, North Korea, and Venezuela—subject to case-by-case waivers. Thus, it was not, as was spun in the media, a total and complete ban without the possibility of case-by-case review.

The state of Hawaii, three individuals, and the Muslim Association of Hawaii argued that Trump exceeded his authority under the Immigration and Nationality Act. They also claimed that his proclamation of the travel ban violated the Establishment Clause of the First Amendment because it was motivated by anti-Muslim bias, not by national security concerns. They could offer no concrete evidence of this. Clearly, they either misunderstood or refused to accept that the president alone has such powers and uses them as he sees necessary to execute proclamations in the protection of the country.

Moreover, in this case, the president's evidence detailed the painstaking process that the administration used to determine which countries to include on the list. It was not, as the liberal media would have you believe, a simple exercise led by Stephen Bannon and Stephen Miller. Instead, the secretary of the Department of Homeland Security was careful and methodical. He first looked at the fundamentals and measured nearly two hundred countries against those fundamentals.

---

[12] "Democrats upset with Supreme Court upholding travel ban," Daniella Diaz and Manu Raju, CNN.com, June 26, 2018, https://www.cnn.com/2018/06/26/politics/congress-travel-ban-reaction-supreme-court/index.html

At the end of this process, the administration found sixteen countries to be extremely troubling and thirty-one other countries to be "at risk." The administration then took action by engaging those countries' governments in a security dialogue about deficiencies, after which the administration compiled its final list. Among the concerns: some are state sponsors of terrorism, some are havens for terrorists, some refused to cooperate with the inquiry, and some lacked the institutional capacity to cooperate effectively.

The ban met a constitutional requirement in that it was neutral on its face regarding religion and applied to people of all faiths. And although five of the seven designated countries are majority-Muslim countries (out of forty-nine such countries around the world), the president stated that they were included for national security reasons: either they are havens for terrorists or they were unwilling or unable "to share or validate important information about individuals" needed to vet visa applicants properly.

Chief Justice John Roberts, who wrote the majority opinion joined by Justices Samuel Alito, Clarence Thomas, Neil Gorsuch, and Anthony Kennedy, began by noting that "[u]nder the Immigration and Nationality Act, foreign nationals seeking entry into the United States undergo a vetting process to ensure that they satisfy the numerous requirements for admission."[13] Section 1182(f) of the law, Roberts wrote, vests considerable authority in the president to restrict the entry of aliens whenever he finds that their entry "would be detrimental to the interests of the United States."[14]

---

[13] "2018 Supplement Constitutional Law," Erwin Chemerinsky, https://books.google.com/books?id=f8lmDwAAQBAJ&pg=PA23&lpg=PA23&dq=the+Immigration+and+Nationality+Act,+foreign+nationals+seeking+entry+into+the+United+States+undergo+a+vetting+process+to+ensure+that+they+satisfy+the+numerous+requirements+for+admission

[14] "Trump Lands Big Win as Supreme Court Upholds Travel Ban," John G. Malcolm, June 26, 2018, https://www.dailysignal.com/2018/06/26/trump-lands-big-win-as-supreme-court-upholds-travel-ban/

In this case, Roberts noted, the president "lawfully exercised that discretion based on his findings—following a worldwide, multi-agency review—that entry of the covered aliens would be detrimental to the national interest. And plaintiffs' attempts to identify a conflict with other provisions in the INA, and their appeal to the statute's purposes and legislative history, fail to overcome the clear statutory language."

In rejecting the plaintiffs' argument that the president's findings were insufficient to survive judicial review, Roberts stated that the proposition that such findings should be subject to judicial review in the first place was "questionable," because they pertain to national security, an area in which courts traditionally accord presidents a great deal of deference. Regardless, the majority held that the findings set forth in the president's proclamation were more than sufficient; indeed, Roberts stated, it was "more detailed than any prior order" issued by a president under the law.[15]

In her dissent, Justice Sonia Sotomayor invoked the Supreme Court's infamous decision in *Korematsu v. United States,* in which the justices upheld the constitutionality of President Franklin Roosevelt's order interning Japanese-Americans during World War II. Sotomayor's dissent drew a sharp rebuke from Chief Justice Roberts. He opined that whatever rhetorical advantage the dissent may see in doing so, *Korematsu* had nothing to do with this case.... "[I]t is wholly inapt to liken that morally repugnant order to a facially neutral policy denying certain foreign nationals the privilege of admission."[16]

The chief justice noted that:

"the dissent's reference to Korematsu, however, affords this Court the opportunity to make express what is already obvious: Korematsu

---

[15] Ibid.

[16] "In Travel ban decision, Supreme Court rejects ruling supporting World War II internment," Chris Fuchs, June 26, 2018, https://www.nbcnews.com/news/asian-america/travel-ban-decision-supreme-court-overturns-ruling-supporting-world-war-n886681

was gravely wrong the day it was decided, has been overruled in the court of history, and—to be clear—has no place in law under the Constitution."[17]

As the Supreme Court acknowledged in *Reno v. American-Arab Anti-Discrimination Committee* in 1999, courts are "ill equipped to determine [the] authenticity and utterly unable to assess [the] adequacy" of a president's "reasons for deeming nationals of a particular country a special threat."[18]

Indeed, as the Supreme Court stated in 2010 in *Holder v. Humanitarian Law Project*, "when it comes to collecting evidence and drawing factual inferences" in the area of national security, "the lack of competence on the part of the courts is marked, and respect for the Government's conclusions is appropriate."

In fact, it is presidents who are given primary responsibility for protecting our homeland. Federal judges are not.

In recent years, appointments to SCOTUS, have become increasingly political and many are alarmed by it. President Trump has now appointed two justices to the court thus swinging the ideological position of the court from liberal leaning to conservative leaning. In 2018, the president nominated Brett Kavanaugh to be an associate justice on SCOTUS. The nomination was controversial from the start. Many Democrats were still angry because former President Obama nominated Merrick Garland to SCOTUS and Republicans in charge of the Senate did not bring the nomination to the floor. So once Kavanaugh was nominated, Democrats pounced. They first put forth the argument that he was nominated from a list compiled by conservative

---

[17] "Did the Supreme Court just overrule the Korematsu decision?" Scott Bomboy, *Constitution Daily*, June 26, 2018, https://constitutioncenter.org/blog/did-the-supreme-court-just-overrule-the -korematsu-decision

[18] "Trump Lands Big Win as Supreme Court Upholds Travel Ban," John G. Malcolm, June 26, 2018, https://www.dailysignal.com/2018/06/26/trump-lands-big-win-as-supreme-court-upholds -travel-ban/

organizations. This argument went flat. Next, ranking member of the judiciary committee Diane Feinstein had a letter from July, 2018 in which Dr. Christine Ford claimed that Kavanaugh sexually assaulted her when they were both in high school. She offered no evidence.

The letter was leaked to The Washington Post. Once the letter was leaked, Feinstein admitted that she had the letter and that she did not reveal it to any of her colleagues nor did she question Kavanaugh about it because she wanted to protect Dr. Ford's identity. Of course, her claim simply was not credible. First, the FBI and Congress protect the identity of persons filing claims all the time. Second, she could have asked the justice about the matter in her one on one interview with him. Finally, she could have revealed it to her colleagues. She chose neither.

Instead, she and mainly Democratic members of the committee launched an all-out attack on the justice in the public square. The justice then went on the offense, appearing on Fox News and offering a fierce defense of himself. The Democrats with help from retiring Senator Flake of Arizona, had the FBI background check extended. The extension yielded nothing new and the justice was confirmed. This hearing has energized the Republican base because on live television a hearing for SCOTUS in which the nominee is answering questions about sexual assault that he allegedly committed while they were both in high school and which was never reported to law enforcement. Many saw this as a pure political move by the Democrats which backfired. It was, in my view, an embarrassing display of partisan bickering that put politics over purpose.

This political side-show taught us that the court has become a political background and that Congress cares more about politics than what's good for the Republic.

Conclusion

The Constitution is the document that keeps us together; politics is the reality that divides us. Lawmakers make laws; the courts interpret whether those laws violate the Constitution. But it is not that simple. Increasingly, federal courts are pulling away from an original interpretation of the Constitution and to an activist view, in which courts are making law. Federal courts are an essential part of the American fabric, and so their actions affect a divided America. The solution for division is a return to an original interpretation of the Constitution. We have seen a return to original interpretation in some significant Supreme Court decisions this term.

CHAPTER 9

Criminal Justice Reform: The Long Road to Finding America's Soul

et me first begin by dispelling the myth that conservatives are against criminal justice reform. The majority of true conservatives are not against something before they were for it. We are free-thinking, logical and realistic. We understand that people who have been in the criminal justice system will eventually return to the communities from which they hail. We want to make sure that when they do, they will be productive members of society and not career criminals. We recognize that they criminal justice system is broken. Where we disagree with liberals and or progressives is how to fix those problems and in some cases what the issues even are.

If one were just to read the statistics of the criminal justice system in the United States, one would conclude that America is not a nation of freedom and opportunity. In fact, one may conclude that it is a nation of criminals. The FBI tracks crime statistics via its Uniform Crime Reporting (UCR) Program, using information from more than thirteen thousand law enforcement agencies. Here are some of its findings reported in 2017:

- Data from 2016 shows there were 95,730 rapes reported to law enforcement, based on the UCR's legacy definition.
- Of the violent crimes reported to police in 2016, aggravated assault made up 64.3 percent, while robbery was 26.6 percent. Rape (legacy definition) accounted for 7.7 percent of the violent crimes reported in 2016, and murder made up 1.4 percent.
- About 7.9 million property crimes were reported to the UCR, with losses (excluding arson) of about 15.6 billion dollars.
- Law enforcement agencies made about 10.7 million arrests in 2016 (excluding arrests for traffic violations).[1]

The irony is that we tout our country as being a law-and-order nation. So why do we still have these kinds of numbers? Is the system working? Has the idea of law and order become more of a political tool and pandering than something requiring action? Who is responsible for the law-and-order country's being seen as lawless and orderless? Has all this talk about law and order created a false sense of security and lulled us into ignoring the current state of crime?

In this chapter, I will explore the need for criminal justice reform in modern-day America. In so doing, it is my intention to look critically at the criminal justice reform movement and to make sense out of what has become like so much in D.C.—a political football hijacked by political hacks because they take advantage of the false sense of

---

[1] "FBI Releases Preliminary Semiannual Crime Statistics for 2017," https://www.fbi.gov/news/pressrel/press-releases/fbi-releases-preliminary-semiannual-crime-statistics-for-2017

security that far too many Americans have chosen to live with. Finally, I present workable solutions based on my work in human rights.

What Is Criminal Justice Reform?

Criminal justice reform is designed to examine the current prison system with the goal of correcting sentencing and other areas that have led to overpopulation in the prisons. The reality is that taxpayers are footing the bill for a burgeoning prison population, thus diverting funds from real issues such as infrastructure. Let's be clear: because of overcrowding, nonviolent offenders are placed in cells with career criminals, and it is in taxpayer-funded prisons that they get the tools to descend into the abyss of a more violent life of crime.

Policies like overcrowding cost taxpayers dearly. They also reduce public safety, because they place many petty criminals in prison cells with hardened criminals for lengthy periods of time—and these petty offenders, after exposure to the harshest of criminal tools and tricks of criminal enterprises, are trained at taxpayer expense to rape and pillage American society with reckless abandon. Without significant, outcome-based reform, we may soon find ourselves as the number-one educator of career thugs and criminals. This cannot continue unless we intend to surrender the republic to the criminals we have created.

In the United States, recidivism rates—which measure whether people reoffend within three years of being released from prison—average 40 percent. In a few states, rates hover around 60 percent.

Overregulation: The Mother of Overcriminalization

Americans will be surprised to learn that many of the federal criminal laws on the books were never voted on by Congress. Only in Washington, D.C., can unelected government paper pushers decide what is a crime and what is not. Washington, D.C., has become a place in which one does not have to have the consent of we the people to affect our lives. Instead, the long-term paper pushers have created a culture in which they take on the role of elected officials, and elected officials gladly give up that power. It is part of the reason that our country continues to be so divided.

The search for power is the bane of our existence, and we the people give up that power without much thought. Too many of us have accepted overregulation as an acceptable way of life. When President Trump said we should take our country back, many claimed he was being racist. No, he was talking about taking power from the hands of unelected officials.

Overcriminalization

So what are some of the reasons for overcriminalization?

The regulations are written largely by unelected bureaucrats, who are accountable to no constituency. But if a type of conduct carries a potential prison sentence, those laws ought to be written by individuals who can be voted out of office—not by unelected bureaucrats.

For example, one of the most infamous federal laws was written by the Department of Homeland Security. The regulation prohibits bringing a bicycle into a building of the National Institutes of Health. That regulation is authorized in Section 1315(c) of Title 40 of the U.S. Code, which also criminalizes any "regulation prescribed" pursuant to that provision of law. That is, the violation of any regulation, no matter how trivial, authorized by that particular statute can make you a federal criminal.

Take a close look at the U.S. Code to find many more of these examples.

We often hear the popular call for "Congress to do its job." In the case of criminal justice reform, we have to insist that our members of Congress do. Why should we allow regulations to create crimes?

Criminal lawmaking is within the purview of Congress. So we must insist that Congress do just that. It can use a simple directive to paper pushers requiring that any criminal justice action they take must include a floor vote by Congress before it will be enforceable. This way, the paper pushers can push whatever papers they desire to push; however, such regulations would be unconstitutional if they did not have on-the-record votes by Congress.

Washington, D.C., has become a divided and an overall political city in which the culture is oriented to division and not to solutions. Congresspeople spend so much time grandstanding, preparing for the next election, fundraising, and preparing for the next higher office. Paper pushers have helped create this culture, so they benefit from it. So while Congress abdicates, the paper pushers celebrate. It is time that Congress takes the issue of the criminal justice system back into its hands. There will be no reform until Congress does so. We the people have also abdicated our responsibility to hold Congress accountable, and are all too happy to allow the criminal justice system to cost us valuable taxpayer dollars, while we do nothing about it.

But understand that this issue is not simply about overregulation. It is about the creation in D.C. of a highly toxic administrative state. I can hear the booming dramatic voices of my critics saying that I am using the term "administrative state" as a pejorative, as most conservatives do to distract from the issue. No, I am using the term because in fact, paper pushers have more influence in the "state" that they have built and profit from than the rest of us. They have become, in many ways, a divisive and highly political band of merry men with political ambitions and political power who have taken it upon themselves to govern because Congress refuses to do its job.

Those who argue that my argument that the administrative state is constitutional ought to read the opinions by justice Clarence Thomas on this very subject—for example:

- In *Department of Transportation v. Association of American Railroads*, Justice Thomas described the violence done to the structure of our constitutional system when Congress delegates its lawmaking powers to administrative agencies.

- In *B&B Hardware v. Hargis Industries*, he stressed that agencies may not, consistent with Article III of the Constitution, usurp the federal courts' judicial power.

- And in *Perez v. Mortgage Bankers Association* and *Michigan v. Environmental Protection Agency*, he argued that federal courts shirk their constitutional duty when they defer to an agency's interpretation of federal law.

Before Justice Thomas, chief justice John Marshall made clear that while paper pushers had the ability to put forth rules on "important" subjects, which is strictly a legislative function, they delegated power to others "to fill up the details."[2]

The paper pushers and the lazy congresspeople got it wrong on this. They have perverted the meaning and twisted it to fit their own political agendas.

Why Criminal Justice Reform?

So that you understand: I am not one who believes in lawlessness. In fact, the opposite is true. I believe that violent people and wanton criminals should never see the light of day. I also do not believe that taxpayers should pay for a system that creates violent criminals. Our current criminal justice system does just that. The notion that our system is for the purpose of rehabilitating criminals is a joke. Let's also remember that a person who is jailed for committing a crime and is branded a criminal is virtually unemployable forever. Thus, many

---

[2] *Marbury v. Madison* (1803), https://usa.usembassy.de/etexts/democrac/9.htm

of those people will turn to the life they learned in prison, as better criminals.

We conservatives have no reason in the world to reject sentencing reform:

> *"[Criminal justice reform is] about basing our laws, our court procedures, and our prison systems on a clear-eyed understanding of human nature—of man's predilection toward sin and his capacity for redemption—along with an uncompromising commitment to human dignity.*
>
> *Respect for the equal dignity of all human life, no matter how small or weak, and for the redemptive capacity of all sinners, no matter how calloused, is the foundation for everything that conservatives stand for. Our approach to policing and punishment should be no different. So, as I see it, criminal justice reform properly understood represents principled conservatism at its best.*
>
> *For conservatives, the question isn't whether we punish those who break the law, but how we punish them—for how long, under what circumstances, and toward what end. Just as the government has the power to punish those who break the law, it has a corresponding duty to use its coercive powers responsibly—to sentence offenders on an individualized basis and no longer than necessary."*[3]

We conservatives have a tendency that is so frustrating and dangerous not only to our cause but to the soul of the republic. We tend to cede issues to the left as if we are so afraid of them because there are no conservative principles involved. We have ceded issues of race, poverty, welfare reform, and so many more because we have not reached deep into our souls and stood by our principles.

---

[3] "The Conservative Case for Criminal Justice Reform," Sen. Mike Lee (R-UT), remarks at The Heritage Foundation, Oct. 7, 2015, thefederalist.com, http://thefederalist.com/2015/10/07/the-conservative-case-for-criminal-justice-reform/

The result is that we have allowed the left to demonize us on so many issues where we hold the high moral ground. And so rather than heal the nation, we retreat into our own little corners and allow the left to bludgeon us with issues that we conservatives can and should lead on. Morality is at the heart of all we do. We exist to use our moral compass to guide a deeply divided nation, yet we flinch.

Criminal justice reform is, at its core, conservative. Yet we fail to plainly explain the difference between providing cover for criminals and a system that promotes treatment of the full human soul. America is divided, and we know that. Yet on the issue of criminal justice reform, we sit back as shrinking violets while the nation bleeds. Criminal justice reform is a divisive issue in part because we have not fully embraced the issue and drawn the battle lines. We have been forced into reactive mode, a tactic that liberals have become so effective at using, and we put our proverbial tails between our legs.

Patriots know the difference between right and wrong, and criminal justice reform is right. Why should we accept being painted with a brush that provides us with a false choice? To believe that picture, we would have to believe that at the heart of the criminal justice question is whether we punish criminals. No conservative doesn't want to punish people who break the law; that is laughable. Thus, to paint criminal justice reform that way is inaccurate and political.

What we are examining in criminal justice reform is whether our current system adequately punishes a person who breaks the law. We also want to examine the issue based on factors such as the severity of the crime and the time criminals should spend in prison. As I wrote earlier, the system has broken down dramatically, given the number of criminals it has created and the number of times they have returned to prison, at a significant cost to taxpayers. The question isn't *whether* we punish those who break the law, but *how* we punish them—for how long, under what circumstances, and toward what end.

The track record of our criminal justice system as created by a subversive administrative state and a lazy, do-nothing Congress is dismal. We have allowed conservative principles to be absent from the discussion and the action because we have decided to cede the moral ground on this issue to those on the left, who not only have eviscerated us in the public square but have demanded their policies be enacted, while too many conservatives have looked the other way. We choose to believe the left's hype while sacrificing our own principles.

So how do we fix the problem? Where do we start? What measures do we use and what outcomes do we want? How do we avoid being part of the problem and ignoring the solution?

What Do We Know About the Current Criminal Justice System?

Try conducting a search on the criminal justice system in the United States to find easily accessible and consumable information on the current issues and challenges facing the system. What you will find is a morass of opinions, conflicting narratives, and a massive set of federal and state regulations that are duplicative, contradictory, and simply unintelligible.

You will also find many political discussions that are "spin" (that is, devoid of facts), partisan approaches, and partisan "solutions" that do no more than drive a wedge through an already divided America. You will also find rules, regulations, and plain nonsense written by a vast, unelected, paper-pushing administrative state that will refer you to websites, codes, and other useless places of "interest" that are designed to frustrate one so that one simply tries to look for the Cliffs Notes version.

For example, in my research for this book, I wanted to know precisely how many crimes were on the books in the federal code. Not surprisingly, I was unable to find out. That information is not available.

So if one cannot even find out how many federal crimes there are, how can it be said that there is little need for criminal justice reform?

And, while Congress has acted to introduce bills on criminal justice reform, it has done nothing significant. As is the case in the paper-pusher culture of Washington, D.C., it has passed nothing. The combination of the administrative state aided by a do-nothing Congress has thrown criminal justice into a highly immoral and fundamentally flawed approach to addressing criminality in the United States.

The administrative state prefers that we are a country of men, not laws. And to date, it has gotten its wish, while we have abdicated our moral duty and responsibility to self-anointed buffoons whose agenda is the maintenance of their power. Country be damned.

The Sentencing and Corrections Reform Act

Having heard the criticisms about the need for a significant and long-lasting change in the criminal justice system, Congress finally introduced the Sentencing Reform and Corrections Act in 2017. But, as is always the case in Washington, the politics of the day resulted in the act being held up in Congress and not passed. The essence of the act appears below.

More specifically, the proposals would take into consideration whether one committing a crime may reduce his or her sentence or change his or her conditions of confinement. There are specific criteria that go along with such consideration:

- Expanding prison programs that are likely to reduce the risk of recidivism, such as educational, job-skills, mental health, and substance-abuse programs
- Encouraging inmates to avail themselves of those programs

- Along with using needs- and risk-assessment tools, matching inmates with programs based on their needs and providing incentives such as the prospect of early release to low- and moderate-risk inmates, and other benefits for high-risk inmates, who complete such programs.

The major proposals currently being considered by Congress are:

- The Corrections Oversight, Recidivism Reduction, and Eliminating Costs for Taxpayers in Our National System (CORRECTIONS) Act of 2015
- The Recidivism Risk Reduction Act
- Portions of the Safe, Accountable, Fair, and Effective (SAFE) Justice Act

These proposals were held up by the Obama administration and its congressional colleagues beginning in 2015. In addition, liberals have prioritized the release of drug dealers over true reform. Republicans have insisted that any change must include a *mens rea* requirement in order to be both effective and fundamentally viable to move forward.

Mens Rea

Put simply, *mens rea* means that the prosecution must prove not only the elements of the crime but that the defendant had a guilty mind. It is this provision that has stalled criminal justice reform for all of this time. The so-called default provision insisted upon by Republicans has fallen on deaf left ears. Branding someone a criminal without determining whether he or she had a guilty mind is fundamentally unfair and patently unjust. Significant *mens rea* reform is crucial to significantly and meaningfully addressing the real issues of reform and the serious and growing problem of unknowing and unwitting individuals and entities violating obscure or unknowable regulations and being branded as criminals.

A major problem with the American criminal justice system is the federal sentencing guidelines. Besides creating a structure for determining sentences, the guidelines help assess resources for the possible prison populations. Federal guidelines estimate how many may go to prison so the U.S. Sentencing Commission (USSC) can request funds to provide additional beds or build new structures. States may look to control prison populations by assessing other options, such as treatment instead of prison for people convicted of driving under the influence of alcohol or other drugs (DUIs). By providing some uniformity, it is assumed it is easier to plan for the future and assure equality when issuing sentences.

Effects on Sentencing

The federal sentencing guidelines are suggestions, not mandatory rules. While they were once considered mandatory, case law deemed strict adherence to them unconstitutional. Judges are supposed to consider specific facts of the case when deciding on a sentence, and the guidelines interfere with that process.

We have federal sentencing laws that too often prohibit judges from exercising their human and legal judgment while punishing offenders. And we have a penal system that isolates offenders from the only people and responsibilities in their life who have the power to facilitate true rehabilitation and redemption. No wonder an estimated three-quarters of offenders released from prison every year are rearrested within five years.

Just as the government has the power to punish those who break the law, it has a corresponding duty to use its coercive powers responsibly—to sentence offenders on an individualized basis and to keep them in prison no longer than necessary.

SENTENCING TABLE
(in months of imprisonment)

	Offense Level	Criminal History Category (Criminal History Points)					
		I (0 or 1)	II (2 or 3)	III (4, 5, 6)	IV (7, 8, 9)	V (10, 11, 12)	VI (13 or more)
Zone A	1	0–6	0–6	0–6	0–6	0–6	0–6
	2	0–6	0–6	0–6	0–6	0–6	1–7
	3	0–6	0–6	0–6	0–6	2–8	3–9
	4	0–6	0–6	0–6	2–8	4–10	6–12
	5	0–6	0–6	1–7	4–10	6–12	9–15
	6	0–6	1–7	2–8	6–12	9–15	12–18
	7	0–6	2–8	4–10	8–14	12–18	15–21
	8	0–6	4–10	6–12	10–16	15–21	18–24
Zone B	9	4–10	6–12	8–14	12–18	18–24	21–27
	10	6–12	8–14	10–16	15–21	21–27	24–30
	11	8–14	10–16	12–18	18–24	24–30	27–33
Zone C	12	10–16	12–18	15–21	21–27	27–33	30–37
	13	12–18	15–21	18–24	24–30	30–37	33–41
	14	15–21	18–24	21–27	27–33	33–41	37–46
	15	18–24	21–27	24–30	30–37	37–46	41–51
	16	21–27	24–30	27–33	33–41	41–51	46–57
	17	24–30	27–33	30–37	37–46	46–57	51–63
	18	27–33	30–37	33–41	41–51	51–63	57–71
	19	30–37	33–41	37–46	46–57	57–71	63–78
	20	33–41	37–46	41–51	51–63	63–78	70–87

Source: United States Sentencing Commission, Guidelines Manual, Chapter X, Part X (November 2016)[4]

In order to preserve the moral authority of our legal system and engender respect for the rule of law, we should be especially careful before enacting laws or promulgating regulations that could cause an individual to be unfairly branded as a criminal.

The debate over criminal justice reform has become bogged down by the nasty divisive politics that now rule America. In our country, name-calling, shouting, and uncivil behavior have replaced morality and our ability to solve vexing problems such as criminal justice and the need for reform. This is not good news for the republic.

---

[4] United States Sentencing Commission, Guidelines Manual, Chapter X, Part X (Nov. 2016), https://www.ussc.gov/guidelines/2016-guidelines-manual/2016-chapter-5

First, the criminal justice system is broken, and we refuse to fix it. Instead, we choose to assign blame while the system gets worse. And we are a great nation?

Second, we refuse to do anything to eradicate the administrative state that we have allowed to survive and thrive. Instead, Congress has abdicated its power on criminal justice reform to those who are running a system that itself needs reform.

Third, an honest analysis of the criminal justice system tells us that a significant number of people released from prison return. When they return, many are hooked on drugs, have medical issues, and/or have mental issues, to name a few possibilities. As we have spent untold amounts of taxpayer dollars keeping them in jail without providing the necessary treatments for what ails them, we now spend even more to fix a problem we created and/or made worse.

Yes, prison is meant to punish. It is, however, not made to do what we are doing: creating more hard-core criminals and then burdening Americans with the effects of crime and weakening their sense of security. While people are in prison, we have a captive audience. Why not begin treating them then? We are already spending taxpayer dollars on them; why not have that spending be more efficient by teaching offenders how to be more productive members of society and to treat their medical, mental, and physical needs? The current criminal justice system is a crime-producing factory, and Congress has not held it responsible for creating more criminals. Instead, Congress rewards the system by providing funds and expecting nothing in return. It is the classic definition of insanity: doing the same thing the same way over and over and expecting different results.

Congress should turn to the states for examples of reform.

"On December 22, 2015, Michigan Governor Rick Snyder approved a law that passed unanimously through the legislature, which create[d]

the presumption that when a criminal law does not specify a 'culpable mental state,' prosecutors must prove a defendant acted 'purposely, knowingly or recklessly.'"[5]

"For that reason, in 2015, Michigan lawmakers establishe[d] that if a law does not indicate whether a 'culpable mental state' ('mens rea') is required to establish guilt, the presumption will be that this is required, meaning that prosecutors must show that the defendant violated the law 'purposely, knowingly or recklessly.'"[6]

"This presumption would not apply if a law explicitly establishes a 'strict liability' standard, or to a drug crime or other offense 'listed in the state penal code, which cover[s] actions that reasonable people already recognize as wrongful or know are illegal.'"[7]

"The Ohio House and Senate also unanimously passed a bill, signed into law by Governor John Kasich on December 19, 2014, that requires lawmakers to assess the state's criminal code before passing new criminal legislation and to specify a mens rea in any new criminal laws (or else explicitly state that intent is not necessary for proof of conviction); the law also provides that a default standard of 'recklessly' should be applied to existing criminal offenses that fail to specify a mens rea requirement."[8]

This shows that states have decided wisely not to wait on the federal government to act or even to demonstrate leadership on criminal justice reform. Instead, states have decided that reforming a system that costs trillions of dollars while getting nothing in return except for more hardened criminals is not good for the states and their citizens. Reform requires the kind of courage that states possess and the federal

---

[5] "Seven State Criminal Justice Reform Measures for Congress to Consider," Legal Memorandum No. 187, Nov. 2, 2016, John-Michael Seibler, published by The Heritage Foundation, http://report.heritage.org/lm187; also http://www.michiganvotes.org/Legislation.aspx? ID=169833

[6] Ibid.

[7] Ibid.

[8] Ibid.; also "Ohio Leads the Way on Criminal Intent Reform," Anne Schieber Dykstra, Capcon, Dec. 24, 2014, https://www.michigancapitolconfidential.com/20850

government lacks. It requires that we all step back from the brinkmanship and the kind of fire-and-brimstone language that now passes for policy-making in our republic. The more bellicose and divided we are, the more criminals we give aid and comfort to. The government has a responsibility to lock prisoners up, and it has an equal responsibility to ensure that the taxpayer dollars used to lock them up do not make the problem worse. Yet we have allowed the government to make the problem worse and are perfectly happy to allow it to keep doing so at a grave cost to the republic.

According to the Pew Center on the States, state and federal spending on corrections has grown 400 percent over the past twenty years, from about twelve billion dollars to about sixty billion dollars.[9] Corrections spending is currently among the fastest-growing line item in state budgets, and one in eight full-time state government employees works in corrections.[10] Yet we conservatives continue to come slowly to the party on reform. Why? Is it because we embrace the stereotype that reforming criminal justice means that we are soft on crime? We are being soft on crime if we do not act affirmatively to attack an out-of-control criminal justice system that is becoming more lawless than the criminals we are seeking to protect the nation from.

To be sure, liberals bear significant responsibility for the current tattered and dysfunctional state of our criminal justice system. In their view, drug dealers and those accused of drug-related crimes should be first priority in the reform of our criminal justice system. While I am not excluding people who have committed such crimes from the list, I am exposing one of the major problems we have in a divided America: sabotage of what is good for the republic versus what is politically expedient. Democrats have seized control of the issue of criminal justice in an effort to paint Republicans as anti-justice. In fact, they

---

[9] "The Criminal Justice Challenge," http://rightoncrime.com/the-criminal-justice-challenge/
[10] Ibid.

have so weaponized criminal justice that the debate is no longer about reform. Instead, it is about politics. They have no interest in reform, because they believe that significant and substantive reform will rob them of the division they need to keep them relevant.

Democrats have seized on the Black Lives Matter movement to further demonize Republicans. In their view, any reform must include a discussion of the relationship between the police and the shooting of unarmed black men. The issue, in their view, is that Republicans want criminal justice reform but don't want to address racism. Coupling the two topics is a deliberate attempt to keep the division going and to never resolve it.

At the heart of a long-term, sustained reform effort is the need to look at the issues that affect the system, including overregulation and overcriminalization. There is also the issue of the American value of morality, by which we treat all people as complete people without regard to factors such as race. Local police, their training, and their interaction with the communities they serve are best dealt with at the local level.

Further, criminal justice reform has nothing to do with resolving whatever issues liberals believe are happening with BLM and law enforcement. It makes no sense that Democrats refuse to accept a very simple, logical conclusion. High rates of incarceration are a national security issue because the federal government is not a bank with unlimited resources. At some point, we will have to make a choice to reduce prison spending, meaning that prisoners—some of whom will be career criminals—will spill into the streets. If Democrats and liberals are comfortable with this, then so be it. However, conservatives will not stand idly by while criminal justice reform goes down the drain.

Let me be much more precise about what I am talking about. As fiscal stalwarts, we believe there should be formulas that are outcome-based that we can rely on in order to justify spending taxpayer dollars. Thus, we are increasingly becoming attracted to performance-incentive funding. The strategy goes something like this: governments should fund prisons (and community corrections programs, for that matter) based on outcomes achieved, not merely on the number of people incarcerated. A government that contracts for lower recidivism rates and increased restitution payments to victims is more likely to find that its prisons are encouraging education and job training behind bars. People from the business world who are more concerned with results than with ideologies are likely to understand this truth intuitively: there is a direct correlation between the money you spend, the outcomes you measure, and the accountability metrics you put in place. You are not measuring ideology, political grandstanding, or political gain. You are measuring *results*.

Conclusion

Criminal justice reform is an idea that has failed in large part because elected officials have delegated responsibility for its efficacy to paper pushers in Washington, D.C. Also, elected officials keep funding an administrative state that creates so many regulations that they then have to create regulations to explain the regulations. Congress has not linked spending to a reduction in incarceration or recidivism. The issue is a political football that has maintained the status quo while undermining an effective criminal justice system.

The solution for criminal justice reform is to involve all parties in an earnest discussion of the issues. Ideological agendas must be excluded from the conversation, outcomes are a must, measures are a must, and taxpayer dollars and how they are spent must be an earnest part of the conversation.

CHAPTER 10

The 2020 Election:
Soul Healer or Soul Stopper?

In 2016, Donald Trump was elected president and everything in America changed. Regardless of what you think of Trump, he did not create a divided America. He walked into one.

In 2020, Trump is widely expected to seek re-election. Of course, this is politics, and anything can change. The question is, what will the next president do to help end division and reclaim America's soul? To be sure, I am not a believer in big government, blue-ribbon commissions, or any other useless entities that exist to make us feel better about ourselves. I believe that we the people bear responsibility for realizing that we are in a deep state of division and that such a deep state of division will eventually make the republic collapse.

We should not look to elected officials to help safeguard our liberty. They are not God on earth and cannot and will not help eradicate the division. The 2020 election is, of course, about electing a president and a Congress for whom job one must be ensuring that our three separate branches of government enact policies and court decisions that do not lead to tyranny. God knows we are dangerously close to tyranny with a profound lack of respect for the Constitution and its meaning, a morally corrupt federal government, political self-dealing, and a lobbying machine that determines what is best for us, the people.

We Americans are so deeply divided along ideological lines that we cannot see how this division affects the republic. Our children are so uneducated about basic American history and civics that it is laughable. Our public education system is a massive failure, where seniority and not competence rules. Far too many of us do not hold elected officials accountable for what we send them to Washington to do. We live in glass houses, yet we throw stones. The republic is becoming a huge glass house, and if the division continues, it will be so pelted with stones that we can no longer stand divided.

In 2020, Americans will shave what it takes to eradicate the division and heal America's soul?

Racial Division

Ever since the days of slavery in America, the country has been divided by race. America is no stranger to racial division. Elected officials such as Bull Connor used the full power of the state to sow racial division:

"A Democrat, in 1961, during the Freedom Rides, Connor ordered Birmingham police to stay away from the bus station while Klansmen attacked the arriving buses and Freedom Riders. In April of 1963, Martin Luther King, Jr. and the Southern Christian Leadership Conference (SCLC) decided to focus their civil rights efforts on Birmingham. On May 2nd, as part of these efforts, more than 1,000 students ranging in age from 8 to 18 left school and

gathered at the 16th Street Baptist Church, intending to march downtown. By the end of the day, 1,200 children had been arrested. On May 3rd, another 1,000 students gathered to march in protest. Connor ordered the use of fire hoses and attack dogs to disperse the marchers, eventually incarcerating over 3,000 demonstrators. These brutal tactics helped focus national attention on the civil rights movement."[1]

This behavior helped cement racism into the fabric of America. While much has changed since then, many Americans believe that the issue of race has never been fully addressed by America, and so the division has continued. Some believe America needs to apologize for slavery and that until it does, racism will continue to be part of America.

The fact is that America *has* apologized for slavery. The U.S. House of Representatives issued an unprecedented apology to black Americans for the institution of slavery, and for the subsequent Jim Crow laws that for years discriminated against blacks as second-class citizens in American society. Despite this and other apologies, race is still a deeply divisive topic in modern-day America. In fact, trafficking in race is a cottage industry in America, and race has become the weapon of choice against people who do not agree that race is the cause of all that ails those who are other than white.

In order to get rid of the division caused by ideological views of race, the 2020 election must address the issue head-on. That is, we the people must ensure that we examine and challenge all the views of candidates running for election in the next season. The reality is, however, that this will not happen. The existence or absence of racism is a weapon in the American psyche, and politicians and some Americans

---

[1] "Theophilus Eugene 'Bull' Connor (1897-1973)," National Park Service, https://www.nps.gov/people/bull-connor.htm

realize there is currency in holding on to that weapon. So despite the fact that this desire to continue to traffic in race will continue to divide the republic, too many will simply take division over solutions. They believe, wrongfully, that it is the job of elected officials to solve racial issues, even though they know that elected officials will not touch this radioactive issue, nor will they address it directly from all sides. We elect those who represent our values, and if our values are divisive ones (in which case they are no values at all), we will get divisive results and will be perfectly fine with division. But will a divided republic stand?

Illegal Immigration

The 2020 election is crucial to solving the issue of illegal immigration. Democrats, in their approach to this issue, have made it clear that they prefer the "rights" of illegal immigrants over those of Americans. The Democratic-controlled state of California enacted laws limiting the ability of state officials to assist federal immigration officers, which has prompted a lawsuit from the Department of Justice for "intentionally obstructing and discriminating against the enforcement of federal immigration law."[2]

But why do Democrats prefer illegals over Americans? It's all politics. They have been unable to attract new voters to the party because their message is all about hating the president. Their policies are out of touch with the majority of Americans. Their party seems to believe that dependency should be a way of life. Since they are unable to get the majority of Americans to buy what they are selling, Democrats have decided that illegal immigration will result in a stronger base and that amnesty is the way to go. In fact, the city of San Francisco has

---

[2] "Democrats Back Illegal Immigrants, Attack Immigration Law Enforcement," Immigration Reform," GOP.com, May 2, 2018, https://gop.com/democrats-back-illegal-immigrants-attack-immigration-law-enforcement-rsr/

already gone down the path of allowing illegal immigrants to vote in school board elections.

The use of the phrase "comprehensive immigration reform" is itself part of the problem. It is, in my view, a politically correct phrase that means nothing. Instead, immigration and its patchwork of laws must be fixed by election 2020 to avoid further division. The solution cannot be a paper-pushing, top-heavy one. Rather, it has to be one that truly exposes the issue without using a politically correct cover. In short, it must be practical. It is therefore a fool's errand to attempt to put in place one so-called comprehensive piece of legislation. Elected officials and their minions cannot solve a simple problem in one bill, yet some are asking that they solve a complex and vexing problem in a "comprehensive" bill. Nonsense.

Election 2020 should be about ensuring that the United States takes full control of our borders. Anything else is not acceptable and will worsen the division. The question of building fences and/or walls has turned into political football. Let's stop that stupid distraction. The fact is that fences and/or walls should be built where it is practical to do so with consideration of geography. Where it is not practical, we must look to the use of technology: virtual barriers could be erected by using unmanned aerial vehicles and cameras and sensors to enhance monitoring and detection.

Let us call illegal immigration out for what it is: a threat to national security. The constant drivel in the media about racism because we need to control our borders must be met head-on and without apology—unless we believe that there is currency in division and are willing to continue to sell our soul for divisive politics. Election 2020 has to be about ensuring that the question of illegal immigration is answered with solutions, not foolish talk and no action.

Working in concert with the measures outlined above is the need to examine how effective domestic law enforcement is in curbing illegal immigration. It is common sense that illegal immigration is due in large part by the now accepted U.S. practice of using illegal labor. Thus, in 2020, we must elect officials who will ensure that employers who hire illegal immigrants face significant fines.

The use of illegal labor here is a huge draw for illegal immigrants, and discouraging it requires telling American employers that there will be consequences for hiring illegal immigrants. I am not talking about creating new tools; we already have Social Security "no match," random workplace inspections, E-Verify, and checks of I-9 forms. However, given the corrupt swamp and its lobbying culture, the tools are not properly used by domestic law enforcement. Big business has and continues to use its campaign cash to defeat any significant efforts to hold employers responsible. Yet we send the same lawmakers back to Congress, and division continues to flourish unabated.

There is theory and there is reality. The American economy is robust, and to keep it that way, we do need foreign workers. So having a temporary worker program in and of itself is a workable solution. The problem is that the current temporary worker system is anything but temporary and is sometimes used as an illegal way of staying in this country. A temporary worker program could supply a rotating, temporary foreign workforce, depending on the demands of the economy. This not only makes economic sense but would channel foreign workers into a legal system, discouraging them from taking an illegal route.

Eradicating a divided America and getting rid of the wedge issue of immigration does not mean getting rid of immigration to America in all forms. It means that we eradicate illegal immigration while making immigration legal and responsive to the needs of Americans. The inefficiencies of the bureaucratic system that manages immigration today are a major reason why we have so many illegal immigrants in the first place.

Liberal Universities

A liberal education was originally designed to have students come together to discuss and analyze issues while learning from one another. It used to mean healthy debate and logical conversations on topics, from which came decisions that students made for themselves. Liberal education was a forum in which there was a free exchange of ideas.

Over the past few decades, too many college campuses have turned the idea of liberal education on its head. Thus, they now traffic in division rather than in education. The problem is that college graduates go on to lead businesses and other institutions where division is a way of life. Liberal universities fall in line with the overhyphenation of America:

> *"That's because radical educators have subdivided most university campuses into racial and gender enclaves by creating African-American studies departments, Hispanic studies departments, women's studies departments, and others. Students in those departments learn only about the importance and influence of their individual ethnic group. A "liberal" education often means one that dismisses any conservative ideas."[3]*

Liberal universities will be a sleeper issue in 2020, and I don't expect that much will be said or done about it. But I think it's important to point out that if we are to heal a divided America, we cannot ignore this issue.

Ideological Warfare

Many Americans are concerned about international war with the likes of North Korea and/or Iran. These are grave concerns. However,

---

[3] "Campus Craziness: Commentary, Education," Edwin J. Feulner, Ph.D., The Heritage Foundation, June 26, 2003, https://www.heritage.org/education/commentary/campus-craziness

another issue that will shape the 2020 election is domestic ideological warfare. Figure 10-1 is a graphic representation of the reality of the hardened ideological divide. What it shows is that as a result of the failed policies of the left, ideology plays a major role in how America is organized, no matter whether it is red, purple or blue. It also proves my point that the division did not start with Donald Trump. Rather, it has been brewing for quite some time. A part of what happened in 2016 was that the country took the narrative by the horns and recrafted it with the election of Donald Trump. People voting for Trump believed that America simply was not working and that career politicians were standing in the way of progress. There is no reason to believe this view will change much in 2020.

Figure 10-1. The Ideological Divide Between Liberals and Conservatives[4]

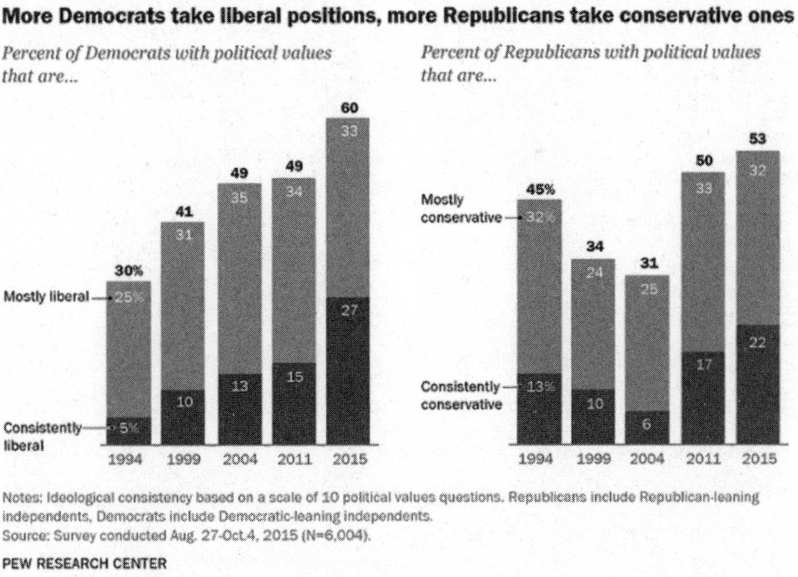
More Democrats take liberal positions, more Republicans take conservative ones
Percent of Democrats with political values that are...
Percent of Republicans with political values that are...
Mostly liberal
Consistently liberal
30%
25%
5%
41
31
10
49
35
13
49
34
15
60
33
27
Mostly conservative
Consistently conservative
45%
32%
13%
34
24
10
31
25
6
50
33
17
53
32
22
1994
1999
2004
2011
2015
Notes: Ideological consistency based on a scale of 10 political values questions. Republicans include Republican-leaning independents, Democrats include Democratic-leaning independents.
Source: Survey conducted Aug. 27-Oct.4, 2015 (N=6,004).
PEW RESEARCH CENTER

[4] "America's Political Divisions in 5 Charts," John Gramlich, Pew Research Center, Washington, D.C., Nov. 7, 2016. http://www.pewresearch.org/fact-tank/2016/11/07/americas-political-divisions-in-5-charts/

Figure 10-2. A Comparison of Presidents' Approval Ratings, from Eisenhower to Obama[5]

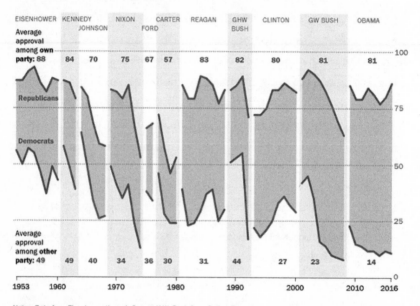

Polarization and presidential approval: Supporters stay loyal, opposition intensifies

% approving of president's job performance, by party

Notes: Data from Eisenhower through George H.W. Bush from Gallup. Because some earlier data did not include partisan leaning, Republicans and Democrats in this graphic do not include leaners.
Source: Survey conducted Oct. 20-25, 2016.

PEW RESEARCH CENTER

The results of the 2016 election are borne out by Figure 10-2. It shows that to win the election, supporters based on party affiliation are most loyal to their choice, despite the foibles of that choice. They will, at all costs, protect that choice and will and do overlook indiscretions made by their choice. While they remain loyal and protective, opposition by the other party intensifies.

---

[5] Ibid.

But intensity without action is the stuff that ideological warfare and division are made of. Hoping for change in 2020 in such ideological trench warfare might be unrealistic. It may take decades to correct.

A major part of the division in America is that Americans have very hardened ideological positions on the domestic issues of the day. There seems to be very little room for compromise, in large part because the left has so perverted so many of the issues that many of us refuse to engage. This refusal to engage has dangerous implications for 2020. The left will paint the Republican party as what is wrong with America. Leftists will insist that America is racist, sexist, anti-immigrant, homophobic, and so on:

> "Mr. Trump's base strategy brands the Republican Party as sexist, racist, xenophobic and anti-immigrant, which magnifies the anti-Trump reaction among Democrats. But it also leaves a tenth who are conservative Catholics and a fifth who are nonreligious conservatives more tentative in their support of the Republican Party—and it pushes away the quarter of Republicans who remain ideologically moderate. The harder the president bangs these drums, the more Democrats become enraged and a segment of Republicans gets demoralized. The more he trashes and defeats his Republican opponents in primaries, the more these voters may contemplate different political options."[6]

But where are the solutions in this quotation? There aren't any. This is naked ideology that will do nothing but encourage a counternarrative from Republicans. In America, every issue, every policy debate, and every idea are seen as being liberal or conservative. The election of Donald Trump is a complete rejection of liberal ideology.

---

[6] "Riling up the Base May Backfire on Trump," Stanley B. Greenberg, *New York Times,* June 18, 2018, https://www.nytimes.com/2018/06/18/opinion/trump-base-midterms-moderate-republicans.html?rref=collection%2Fsectioncollection%2Fopinion

Liberals simply do not understand that their underlying view that all things are possible through government is patently false and unacceptable. The American people at large have returned to the practical position that the existing order of society plus strong laws, leadership institutions, and strict moral codes are in part what makes a nation great. American politics today has an ideology. The winning ideology —the right ideology—is based on a solid foundation. It rejects the convoluted thinking below:

> *"The lesson is this: in modern American politics, having an ideologically coherent and disciplined party is an advantage, not a liability. This flies in the face of conventional wisdom: during the 2016 primary, many Democrats, especially those who supported Clinton, worried about the 'purism' of the party's younger and more progressive wing: would it force the party to confront a choice between nominating ideologically progressive candidates who would be unelectable and facing mass defections to its left? After all, it was widely understood that candidates needed to 'pivot to the center' to win general elections. Clinton's claim to be a 'progressive who gets things done' was founded on this assumption: the notion was that Sanders' policies, even if you found them desirable, were unlikely to get done because it was too extreme, while Clinton's was closer to the center and therefore more achievable. Yet in 2017 the most extreme political party in decades seems poised to get more things done than any party since the Johnson administration. What's wrong with the conventional view?"[7]*

These two competing ideological positions demonstrate exactly why we are set up in 2020 for ideological warfare. The left has drawn a line in the sand on ideology, and the right has responded. The problem

---

[7] "Why Republicans Are Impressive," Michael Kinnucan, Current Affairs, Jan. 28, 2017, https://www.currentaffairs.org/2017/01/why-republicans-are-impressive

with the left's position is that it does not at all deal with the issues that divide the republic. Instead, leftists have aimed their fire directly at President Trump. They are arguing that Americans should vote for their party because Trump is a Republican, not a Democrat. They are also attempting to relitigate 2016 in hopes of winning 2020.

And where is the beef in their arguments? The left fails to understand that naked ideology is not a strategy to solve America's division. It is a divisive and deliberate attempt to stoke an ideological war. Leftists are unwilling to offer substance and address the issues that cause a divided America. It is as if they are spoiling for an ideological war that they cannot win. The left has created an America in which thinking for ourselves is a disability, in which individual identity is more important than American identity, and in which babbling and shouting take the place of logical and well-reasoned arguments.

In 2020, all sides must be sure they are seeking solutions and not just scoring points. We have to insist that 2020 is not fought merely on ideological grounds. It is time that we ask the left to look honestly at its failed policies and its disastrous penchant to force us to live in an America that seeks to respect differences for no other reason than the fact that we are different from one another.

Yes, we are different. We are also American, so the starting point to healing America is to realize that we are Americans first. It as if we have forgotten what it means to be American. Although Americans look different and have different socioeconomic statuses, we still are guided by the Constitution. It is what has held us together through war, strife, and corruption. We have not built a nation on being different; we have built it based on being cohesive, where the only issue is being proud Americans.

The battle for our soul is a battle for the values and morals that have made America great; it is not for what has made America different.

Dateline: The U.S. Census

The immigration debate became ugly when the Trump administration announced that it would add a question to the 2020 census asking respondents about their citizenship status. The ideological flame was turned up to blazing. Liberals lost their collective minds. New York and California immediately filed lawsuits. However, the leftists are simply crying wolf. This question has been asked on the census before, and regardless of whether people answer the question or not, they will be counted. This is, as usual, a naked ideological war by the left. This chapter explains the details.

The U.S. secretary of commerce, Wilbur Ross, wrote to the Department of Homeland Security with the following request:

> "As you know, on December 12, 2017, the Department of Justice requested that the Census Bureau reinstate a citizenship question on the decennial census to provide census block level citizenship voting age population [CVAP] data that are not currently available from government survey data.... DOJ and the courts use CVAP data for determining violations of Section 2 of the Voting Rights Act and having these data at the census block level will permit more effective enforcement of the Act. Section 2 protects minority population voting rights.
>
> Following receipt of the DOJ request, I set out to take a hard look at the request and ensure that I considered all facts and data relevant to the question so that I could make an informed decision on how to respond. To that end, the Department of Commerce (Department) immediately initiated a comprehensive review process led by the Census Bureau.
>
> The Department and Census Bureau's review of the DOJ request, as with all significant Census assessments, prioritized the goal of obtaining complete and accurate data. [emphasis added] The decennial census is mandated in the Constitution

200

and its data are relied on for a myriad of important govern-
ment decisions, including apportionment of Congressional seats
among states, enforcement of voting rights laws, and allocation
of federal funds. These are foundational elements of our democ-
racy, and it is therefore incumbent upon the Department and the
Census Bureau to make every effort to provide a complete and
accurate decennial census."[8]

The left went immediately to court:

"'This is a brazen attempt by the Trump administration to cheat
on the census, to undermine the accuracy of the census and to
attack states that have large immigrant populations—states, most
of which just happen to be Democratic states," said Rep. Jerrold
Nadler, Democrat of New York.'"[9]

Furthermore, a lawsuit by California Attorney General Xavier
Becerra contends that if the census undercounted immigrants, it would
be an incomplete population count that violates its constitutional purpose, which is to divide up seats in the U.S. House of Representatives
based on the total U.S. population. (Census numbers also are used to
allocate billions of dollars in federal funds.) The California lawsuit also
says the Trump administration failed to follow government procedures
for adding questions to the decennial census form.[10]

This shows once again the tools of ideological warfare and division
that are products of left-wing ideology.

---

[8] "Reinstatement of a Citizenship Question on the 2020 Decennial Census Questionnaire," memo from secretary of commerce Wilbur Ross to undersecretary for economic affairs Karen Dunn Kelley, March 26, 2018, included as Exhibit 1 in *State of California v. Wilbur L. Ross Jr.*, https://www.documentcloud.org/documents/4423334-California-Complaint-Census.html

[9] "Cities and States Mount Court Challenge to Census Question on Citizenship," Michael Wines, April 3, 2018, https://www.nytimes.com/2018/04/03/us/census-citizenship-question-court-challenge.html

[10] *State of California v. Wilbur L. Ross Jr*, Complaint for Declaratory and Injunctive Relief, filed March 26, 2018, https://www.documentcloud.org/documents/4423334-California-Complaint-Census.html

This is not the first time that the Census Bureau has included the citizenship question. A question about U.S. citizenship status appeared in censuses in 1820 and 1830; in 1870, for males twenty-one years of age and older; and in every census year since 1890 with the exception of 1960, according to 2009 U.S. Census Bureau information. The last time all households were asked about U.S. citizenship was in the 1950 census. That census questioned where individuals were born, and "if foreign-born—is he naturalized?"

So what is wrong with asking the question? The citizenship question does not ask about a person's legal status; its concern is only about citizenship status and thus has nothing whatsoever to do with immigration enforcement. The left knows good and well that federal law prevents census data from being used for anything other than statistical analysis. While advancing the argument that the law has to do with legal status, why have leftists not presented any evidence that federal agencies such as Immigration and Customs Enforcement will use the answers to deport people who are here illegally? This is because they have no such evidence. This is yet another divisive tactic that they believe will play well with their base.

The reality is that the left leaves out the fact that the citizenship question protects minority voters by aiding Texas and other states in apportioning legislative seats while complying with the Voting Rights Act. That law is unwavering in forbidding the "denial or abridgement of the right of any citizen of the United States to vote on account of race or color." Courts have held that this prevents states from drawing legislative districts which dilute minority voting; the left is asking that we forget about accurate citizenship numbers when determining issues of voting rights violations. In the left's view, we should simply rely on a guess.

The entire census question discussion is a pig in a poke. It has no connection to reality; it further demonstrates that the left prefers division over solutions and is trying to win political points by pandering to a base that is uneducated about the census question. The left is afraid that if it educates its base about the census question, it would lose the debate. Its base would realize that:

1. This is not the first time the question has been asked.

2. The left says that responses to individual questions shape overall response rates. There simply is no evidence of this.

3. As a nation, we never have given up the right nor should we give up the right to know about citizenship status. To do so would just be stupid.

4. The Voting Rights Act, which the left claims to loves, requires data about citizenship status. Yet the left doesn't want us to collect it?

On the census question, the left advances its usual playbook: one of drunken pandering with help from the mainstream media. Leftists craft a false narrative on the question, gin up the base without providing facts, and sell the narrative to the media, and the media plays the false narrative over and over. The chattering class opines on how reckless the policy is, and the chasm between Americans grows wider. This behavior by elected officials is akin to organized crime, where power, control, and money rule the day. The difference is that since elected officials make the law, they determine that what they are doing is perfectly legal. As a sovereign nation, America should know what proportion of its population is composed of citizens and what proportion is not. Winning by hoodwinking (the established practice of the left) shows, in my opinion, that the left couldn't care less about America's soul. Instead, it cares about power and control. That power comes with the trappings of the swamp—lavish parties, lobbying junkets, corruption, and self-dealing.

Searching for and finding America's soul are crucial for the survival of the republic. However, when one is more invested in self-gratification by keeping a base uninformed, then that person need not search for America's soul but rather for his or her own.

Call to Action

The race to win the 2020 election and change America has already begun. As Americans, we have to do our own soul-searching. We are deeply divided, and there is a cloud over America's soul. In order for us to heal the division, we must do the following:

- We must admit that America is a great country, and that despite attempts to destroy us from outside and inside, we remain strong.

- We must freely admit that many of our problems are moral ones. Morality, in my view, concerns itself with what is right and what is wrong. We transfer our own sense of morality from generation to generation. We know that a divided America is morally wrong. Morality exists prior to the acceptance or (rejection) of its standards by us Americans. The moral point of view is American, and no one is exempt from it. We must get rid of those laws, practices, policies, and ideologies that continue to make division thrive.

- We need to look at the importance of originalism in Constitutional interpretation. Morality and law have a symbiotic relationship in that they share a concern over policies, principles, and behaviors. When we allow courts to forget about the Constitution and make law based on their own view of morality, we divide America even more. The issue is not whether a judge is a liberal or a conservative, it is how he or she will interpret the Constitution regardless of his or her views.

- As a general matter, we have to seek objective information before making decisions regarding the lawmakers we elect and what is news and what is not. In America, we have allowed the vast majority of the news media to determine what are facts, what are not, and what decisions we should make based on the media's definition of facts. To be sure, not all of America's media is fake. The problem is that too much of it is. By fake, I mean that the persons who are supposed to report the news now decide what the news should be. This is because news today is ego driven. That is, specifically on the issue of politics and as we go into the 2020 election, watch for the news media to select candidates to report on based on how they feel about the candidate, rather than on reason. Expect them to cover stories that highlight division and present spin. Like P. T. Barnum, American news believes that a sucker is born every minute and that those in the American electorate are such suckers, and that they can be easily bamboozled.

- To help get rid of the divide, we Americans must educate ourselves on the candidates and the positions we want them to advance. Do we want candidates who view the division from the vantage point of not interfering with the liberty of others (thus securing the right of liberty) or from the standpoint of providing benefits and or services to certain people (thus securing welfare rights)?

- We must know the issues that are eating at America's soul; that's the only way change will happen in 2020. This means that we must take action that does not simply outsource government to elected officials. When was the last time we held our elected officials truly accountable for anything? How much time do our elected officials spend in the swamp instead of on the ground at home? Are we satisfied with elected officials who merely bring home the bacon to our districts and are corrupt?

- We need to keep in mind our moral point of view. It seems that too many of us have abandoned the moral point of view as a way of solving what is eating at America's soul. Recall what the moral point of view is. It seeks to address issues by reason rather than by mere inclination. However, we live in a nation so corrupted and ruled by political correctness that we have the moral-point-of-view discussion in private. The fact is that invoking emotional responses in eradicating division more often than not evokes emotional responses. Thus, the need to use reason as our guide. It is an appeal to the moral imperative that will help us make sound decisions in 2020. Should we choose this path, we will go a long way toward eliminating division and finding America's long-lost soul.

- We can recognize that there are some fundamental issues we will never agree on. But 2020 requires that we search for those issues we do agree on and work to erase the division.

- In 2020, we need to insist on facts, moral clarity, and solutions, rather than hyperbole. Our division is in part based on the fact that we have become creatures of and slaves to hyperbole.

- In 2020, turn education on its head. Our public education system exists to serve teachers and unions. It no longer exists to educate students.

- We need to return to a focus on families as the fabric that holds us together. Technology has taken over parenting. When was the last time your family had meals together as a family and without electronic devices at the table?

It is clear that this call to action is a beginning and not an end. Passive participation in our republic has led to decay. Too many of us have ceded the moral ground to the elites, the academics, and the politically correct faction of the republic. The time to stop it is now. Our republic is strong, but we all know that a house divided against itself cannot stand. We are that house. We need no longer subscribe to the stupid axiom that we cannot make waves. Making waves and demanding accountability from elected officials in 2020 is the solution.

AFTERWORD

I emigrated from the country of Grenada, a small Caribbean island with a population of one hundred thousand. The privilege of being an American citizen has enriched my life greatly. I wrote this book because the divisions are tearing apart the republic. The failed policies of the left have resulted in our being the worse for wear. It is time that we take control of the republic, lest we cede greatness to other nations.

The initial book proposal I wrote looks very different from this book. This is because I have learned a great deal by being actively involved in the affairs of the republic. Of this, I am proud. I must admit that this was a tough book to write because I was trained as an academic; in academia, big words matter, and involving Dick and Debbie Salt of the Earth in a discussion is largely irrelevant. That academic snobbery is part of the problem. America is made up of people who are different from one another. But being different in and of itself is not the issue. Being American is.

I developed my point of view in large part through vigorous debate with people who were the same as well as people who were different. I spent a bit of time with the Hooligan Squad, an eclectic group of my dad's friends. They taught me how to think through some of the thorniest issues in this book. In writing this book, I hoped to impart some of what I have learned from them. I do not think that we are beyond repair in America. I do think it is time that we had an honest conversation with ourselves about what divides us and why. I fully accept that many liberals and some conservatives will largely criticize my book, but this is the beauty of America, and I fully accept this. As 2020 approaches, I hope that we will all take stock of where we are as a country and be actively engaged for generations to come.

MAY 31, 2019